DAY TRADING MASTERY MADE QUICK AND EASY

Master Essential Techniques In Just 15 Minutes A Day Even If You're Starting From Scratch

---

DANIEL FERNELL

Contents

Introduction

In the fast-paced world of financial markets, day trading is a beacon of opportunity for those looking to dip their toes into trading stocks, currencies, and more. Picture this: You're sitting at your desk, coffee in hand, watching the digital ticker tape roll by, feeling the rush of making split-second decisions that could turn a profit. It sounds thrilling, doesn't it?

But before you dive headfirst into the whirlwind of day trading, let's pause. Is day trading right for you? It's a question that demands a closer look, a bit of introspection, and maybe even a reality check.

Picture this: The sun is barely up, and you're already scanning market charts, analyzing trends, and planning your moves. A day trader's life is a blend of strategy, adrenaline, and yes, occasional moments of frustration. But amidst the ups and downs, there's an undeniable thrill in navigating the financial currents and spotting opportunities that others might miss.

Each day, from managing risk to seizing fleeting opportunities, brings new challenges and potential rewards. It's not just about numbers on a screen; it's about understanding market psychology and leveraging it to your advantage.

Here's a shocking statistic: Nearly 40% of day traders throw in the towel within just one month of starting. The allure of quick gains can quickly fade when faced with the market's unpredictable reality. Furthermore, only 13% of day traders are still in the game within three years of setting foot in the market. So, what separates the dropouts from the success stories?

The key lies in preparation. Day trading isn't just about making quick decisions; it's about making informed ones. Research, practice, and a solid understanding of market dynamics will be your allies on this journey. It's like learning to surf before tackling those big waves—you need skills and knowledge to ride them smoothly.

Day trading can be thrilling, and yes, it can be financially rewarding. But, like any other skill, it takes more than a few lucky guesses or intuition to get there. *Day Trading Mastery Made Quick and Easy* will show you how to navigate the ups, downs, and sideways turns of day trading so you can go from "Wait, what's a candlestick chart?" to "I just had my best trading day ever!"

Whether you're starting with zero experience or have already dipped your toes in the trading pool, this book will help you avoid the common pitfalls beginners face and guide you toward making smarter, more informed decisions.

Let's dive into what you can expect to learn.

We'll explore the realities of what it means to day trade, from the excitement of the highs to the patience required during the lows. You'll also get a sneak peek into a typical day in the life of a day trader. Spoiler alert: It may not be all champagne and caviar, but it will be incredibly rewarding with the right mindset.

You'll learn about setting realistic goals, building a budget, and managing risk. A good day trader knows that risk is always part of the game. However, managing it wisely is what separates the pros from the newbies. We'll talk about how much capital you need to start, how to structure your trading plan, and how to stick to that plan when things get tough.

We'll also dive into the critical tools of the trade—like charts, real-time data feeds, and order types—and discuss how they work together to give you a competitive edge. You'll soon find that your trading room is more than just a desk and a laptop—it's your command center!

Believe it or not, the market can sometimes feel like a battlefield—where your worst enemy is your fear, greed, or impatience. But don't worry; you will be armed with the knowledge and discipline to stay on the safer side of things.

You'll get a solid understanding of the markets and how each one behaves. Should you focus on fast-moving tech stocks or maybe the foreign exchange (Forex) market? We'll help you weigh your options so you can easily decide what suits your risk tolerance, interests, and trading style.

From trading platforms to news sources and charting tools to community forums, we'll ensure you have the proper setup to stay informed, agile, and prepared. After all, in the world of day trading, having the right tools can be the difference between a good day and a not-so-good one.

We'll explore simple and advanced strategies, from scalping (gaining quick, small profits) to momentum trading (riding a trend). No matter your style, you'll find strategies that fit your personality, goals, and risk appetite. We'll ensure you understand how to apply them in real market conditions, not just in theory.

Last but certainly not least, we'll end with a bit of wisdom from those who've been in the trenches and come out victorious. In Chapter Eight, you'll learn from the experiences of the greatest traders in history—people who have turned day trading into an art form.

We'll look at their approaches, their strategies, and most importantly, their mistakes because, let's face it, even industry titans had to deal with a few knocks along the way, and by learning from them, you can avoid some hard knocks yourself.

Day trading isn't a shortcut to riches, but it can be fruitful with the right amount of dedication, discipline, and knowledge. This is your guide—your roadmap to navigating the challenges and seizing the opportunities that the market has to offer. So, are you ready to enter the exciting world of day trading?

ONE

Is Day Trading Right for You?

The goal of a successful trader is to make the best trades. Money is secondary.

Alexander Elder

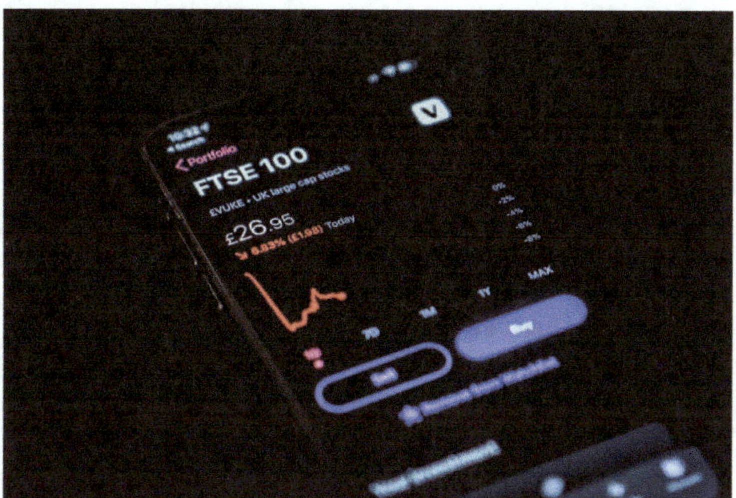

Understanding Day Trading

Day trading is a fast-paced, speculative strategy where traders buy and sell financial instruments, like stocks, options, or currencies, within a single trading day. The objective is to profit from slight price movements, using high volume and volatility to optimize immediate gains. In contrast to long-term investing, day trading is centered on intraday price activity, so positions are closed before the market closes to minimize overnight risks.

Key Features of Day Trading

1. **Frequent Transactions:** Day traders execute multiple trades daily, aiming to profit from minor market fluctuations. This style requires constant monitoring of market movements and technical indicators.
2. **Leverage:** Many day traders use borrowed money (leverage) to magnify potential gains, but this strategy increases the risk of losses. Leverage lets you take larger positions with relatively small capital, amplifying profits and risks.
3. **Short Time Frames:** Day traders operate on short time frames, from seconds to hours, relying on technical analysis and price charts. They avoid holding positions overnight to mitigate exposure to external factors that could affect the market before it opens the next day.
4. **Technical Analysis:** Successful day traders heavily rely on technical analyses like chart patterns, moving averages, and volume indicators. The focus is on

identifying short-term trends and price patterns to make quick decisions.

5. **Market Volatility:** Day trading thrives in volatile markets, where frequent price changes create opportunities for traders. Highly liquid markets with tight spreads, like currency pairs, stocks, and options, are preferred for their rapid price movements.
6. **Risk Management:** Due to the high risks associated with day trading, risk management strategies like stop-loss orders are essential. Traders set predefined levels to exit a losing trade, minimizing potential losses. They also limit their trade sizes and only risk a small portion of their capital per trade.
7. **Discipline and Strategy:** Day trading requires discipline, patience, and adherence to a well-defined trading plan. Traders often specialize in specific markets or instruments and develop strategies suited to their risk tolerance, skill level, and market conditions.

Day trading can be profitable, but it's highly risky and requires significant capital, knowledge, and emotional control. It offers the potential for high rewards, but the possibility of rapid financial loss is real, especially for beginners. Before diving in, consider your financial situation, risk tolerance, and ability to dedicate time and effort to this intensive practice.

Day Trading vs. Alternative Styles

When it comes to trading, day trading and swing trading are your main approaches. Both have appeal but operate on different timelines and strategies.

The Difference Between Day Trading and Swing Trading

- **Day Trading:** It's all about buying and selling within a single day. Day trading is intense and requires quick thinking and decision-making.
- **Pros:** You can avoid overnight risks.
- **Cons:** It's stressful and needs constant attention.
- **Swing Trading:** A more laid-back form of trading where trades can last days or even weeks.
- **Pros:** It's slower but allows for more significant potential gains from market movements.
- **Cons:** You're exposed to overnight risks like market gaps or sudden news that could affect your position.

Why Pick Day Trading Over Swing Trading?

If you're into fast-paced action and can devote time to actively watching the market, day trading could be your jam. It's intense but yields quick results, especially if you thrive on making real-time decisions. Swing trading is less demanding and offers more flexibility, but the slower pace may not be for you.

Ultimately, your trading style depends on your personality, your risk tolerance, and the time you're willing to dedicate. Both styles come with pros and cons, but day trading is the go-to for those who love a fast-paced, action-packed market experience.

Myths or Reality: Debunking Common Misconceptions About Day Trading

Day trading is shrouded in myths, often making it seem either too good or too bad. Let's bust some of those misconceptions (*Don't Fall for These Common Myths about Day Trading*, 2021)!

1. **Day trading is a scam:** Not true! It's a legitimate way to trade, but high risks, flawed strategies, and unverified *coaches* give it a shady rep.
2. **Day trading will make you rich:** Nope. Success comes with skill, patience, and realistic expectations.
3. **No training is needed:** Incorrect. Understanding markets, tools, and strategies is crucial.
4. **Profits are instant:** Far from it—most traders take time to become consistently profitable.
5. **You can make thousands in a single trade:** Occasionally, yes, but it's rare, and risk management is critical.
6. **Once you learn the basics, you'll always make money:** Markets are unpredictable, and ongoing learning is essential.

Should You Quit Your Job to Trade Stocks?

Day trading sounds exciting, right? But before you hand in your resignation, let's look at the potential risks:

Know the Risks

1. **High tax impact:** Day traders can face steep short-term capital gains taxes.
2. **Losing money:** Most traders lose money, especially at the start.
3. **High-stress levels:** The fast-paced nature can be mentally exhausting.
4. **Greater time investment:** Success requires constant monitoring of markets.
5. **High expenses:** Costs like software, commissions, and potential margin interest add up fast.

Careful consideration of these risks can save you headaches (and possibly a lot of money)!

Potential Financial Rewards

1. **No overnight risk:** Day trading is like a chef who finishes cooking before serving dinner. You get to taste and adjust your dish right away, avoiding the surprises that come with letting it sit overnight. You get to close your positions before the market closes, avoiding any surprises the next day.
2. **Be your own boss:** Forget clocking in! You control your trading hours.

3. **Leverage:** Borrowing capital can amplify your gains (but also your losses!). Think of leverage as a friend lifting weights with you.
4. **Mental workout:** Day trading keeps your brain sharp and strategic. It's like a game of chess where each move requires careful thought and planning.
5. **No degree needed**: It's accessible without an expensive education.
6. **Earn Interest:** If you hold cash, you can earn interest while you trade.
7. **Quick learning curve:** Experience comes fast when you're actively trading. It's like learning to ride a bike: The more you practice, the quicker you improve. You'll gain experience faster when you're actively engaged in the market (Sykes, 2018).

The Balancing Act: Navigating Risks and Rewards in Day Trading

Imagine walking a tightrope with gold at the end. That's day trading: A delicate balance between risk and reward.

- The risk-reward ratio is your balancing pole. A 2:1 ratio, for example, means you're risking $1 to make $2—sensible, right? But it's not just about the ratio; it's about managing risks smartly. Stop-loss orders and position sizing can prevent a fall (Hickmann, 2023).
- While rewards can be exciting, overconfidence is the enemy of progress. Keep one foot grounded by constantly assessing your potential rewards and risks—the trick is staying balanced on the rope.

Why Most Day Traders Lose (And How You Can Avoid It)

Let's dive into why most day traders lose money and how you can steer clear of those traps.

1. **Emotional Trading:** Picture yourself in a casino—your heart's racing and you're betting based on gut feelings. Emotional trading is like that—panic or greed drives poor decisions. You must keep your emotions in check and stick to the facts to succeed.
2. **No Risk Management:** Day trading without risk management is like sailing without a life jacket. If a trade goes south, you could lose everything without strategies like stop-loss orders. Successful traders always limit their potential losses.
3. **Lack of Discipline:** Imagine a marathon runner who sprints the first mile and walks the rest. They're not following the plan. Similarly, undisciplined traders might abandon their strategy at the first sign of trouble, missing out on long-term gains. Discipline is vital to staying consistent.
4. **Skipping Technical Analysis:** It's like driving without a map. Without understanding charts, trends, and indicators, you're flying blind in the market. Technical analysis helps traders navigate the highs and lows of the market, increasing their odds of success.
5. **Over-trading:** Think of it like binge eating. Sure, one trade might work out, but overdoing it can lead to losses piling up. More trades don't necessarily mean more profit; smart, selective trades often yield better results.

6. **Unrealistic Expectations**: If you think day trading will make you rich overnight, you're setting yourself up for disappointment. Many traders go in with visions of grandeur, only to face harsh realities. Success comes from long-term effort rather than instant gratification.

Avoiding these pitfalls requires patience, a solid strategy, and constant learning. Managing your emotions, planning your trades, and understanding the market lets you sidestep the common mistakes that cause most traders to lose (*Why Most Traders Lose Money: 24 Surprising Statistics,* 2019).

The Rule book of Day Traders

Before you take action, familiarize yourself with the rules and regulations that govern this financial playground. Think of it as learning the rules of a new game—knowing how to play ensures you stay in the game without risking a penalty or disqualification.

Understanding Regulations

Day trading is like a high-speed race. You want to go fast, but if you don't follow the traffic rules, you might find yourself in a wreck. Here are some regulations to keep in mind:

- **Pattern day trader rule:** If you make four or more day trades within five business days in a margin account, you will be classified as a "pattern day trader." This means you must maintain a minimum balance of $25,000 in your trading account. It's like needing a special license to drive a sports car—you need to prove you can handle the speed!

- **Leverage limits:** Day traders often use leverage to amplify their trades, but be careful, as regulations restrict the amount of leverage you can use based on your account balance. It's like using a trampoline; you want to bounce high but ensure a soft landing. Over-leveraging leads to significant losses.

Brokerage Rules

Every trading platform has rules, so choosing a reputable brokerage that aligns with your trading style is essential. Think of your broker as your coach. They can guide you, but you need to understand their playbook:

- **Commissions and fees:** Be aware of the costs associated with trading. Just like buying ingredients for a recipe, every trade might come with a price tag. Make sure you factor in these costs to calculate your profits accurately.
- **Order types:** Familiarize yourself with different order types, like market, limit, and stop-loss orders. It's like having different tools in a toolbox; each serves a specific purpose and helps you handle various situations effectively.

Requirements for a Successful Start

Now that you have a grasp of the rules, let's talk about the essential requirements to kick off your journey:

- **Education:** Education is your road map. It guides you through the market's twists and turns. Take the time to read books, watch tutorials, or enroll in courses that cover strategies, technical analysis, and market trends.
- **Trading plan:** Create a solid trading plan that outlines your goals, risk tolerance, and strategies. It helps you stay focused and avoid impulsive decisions. Without a plan, you might drift aimlessly like a ship without a rudder.
- **Practice with a demo account:** Before you use real money, practice with a demo account. It's like training wheels for a bike—you learn to balance and ride without the risk of falling. Use this opportunity to test strategies and gain some much-needed confidence.
- **Emotional control:** Day trading can be emotionally taxing, akin to a roller coaster ride. Prepare yourself for the ups and downs by developing emotional discipline. Establish rules for handling losses and profits and stick to your trading plan.

Staying Within Legal Boundaries

Finally, always remember to stay within legal boundaries. Follow the regulations to avoid potential legal issues. It's like adhering to the rules of a game; cheating may provide short-term wins, but it will eventually catch up to you.

When you understand the rules and requirements of day trading, you'll be better equipped to navigate this exciting world and make informed decisions. So, gear up, stay informed, and enjoy the thrill of the trade while playing by the rules!

Your Path to Success: How to Tilt the Odds in Your Favor as a Day Trader

Trading is as exhilarating as it is unpredictable. It's like surfing—when you ride the waves just right, it's thrilling. However, you make one wrong move, and you're wiped out. So, how do you stay on the board and avoid wipe outs? Here's a road map to increase your chances of success:

Knowledge Is Power

Before jumping in, imagine you're about to compete in a chess match. Would you sit down without knowing the rules, hoping to beat your opponent by chance? Of course not! Trading is no different—it's a game where the educated thrive. Start by absorbing as much information as possible: read books, take courses, follow market news, and familiarize yourself with technical analysis. This knowledge becomes your arsenal, helping you make informed decisions instead of trading based on gut feelings.

Set Aside Funds

Think of trading like a trip to the casino (though, hopefully, with better odds). You don't walk into a casino planning to spend your entire savings; similarly, you should allocate specific funds for trading that you're prepared to lose. This "play money" ensures you don't dip into your life savings when things don't go your way. A good rule of thumb? Only trade with what you can afford to lose because, in this fast-paced world, losses happen, and they happen quickly.

Set Aside Time

Trading isn't like a part-time job where you can pop in and out between other tasks. It's more like a high-intensity sport where you must be fully present and focused. Markets move at lightning speed, and you could miss critical opportunities if you're not paying attention. Set aside dedicated time to watch the markets closely. Think of it as an investment not just in money but also in your time.

Start Small

Just as you wouldn't start your fitness journey by trying to bench press 100 pounds, don't start your trading career by throwing massive amounts of money into the market. Start small—test the waters, see what strategies work, and give yourself space to make mistakes without significant financial consequences. Over time, as you build confidence and skill, you can scale up your trades.

Avoid Penny Stocks

Penny stocks seem like a good idea because they're cheap, but in reality, they're the junk food of the stock market. They promise quick rewards but are highly volatile and can burn you faster than you can say "market crash." Instead, stick to stocks that have a solid reputation and history. They may be pricier but offer stability that penny stocks simply can't.

Time Those Trades

Trading is all about timing—like catching the perfect wave when surfing. The opening and closing hours of the stock market are often the most volatile, presenting the best profit opportunities. However, don't rush into trades just because the market is open; be patient and wait for the right conditions to align. Sometimes, sitting on your hands is the smartest move to make.

Cut Losses With Limit Orders

Sometimes, the market won't go your way. It's like setting out for a sunny beach day, only for clouds to appear. That's where limit orders come in. A limit order lets you cut your losses before they spiral out of control. It's like setting an umbrella before the storm hits—planning protects you when the tide turns against you.

Be Realistic About Profits

Finally, keep your expectations grounded. While movies and social media might glamorize traders making thousands of dollars in a few minutes, that's far from the daily reality. Day trading is more of a marathon than a sprint. You can't simply retire after a few trades, but you can build your profits over time with patience and skill. Keep your eyes on the long-term goal rather than trying to hit a home run with every trade.

Success isn't just about making money—it's about preparing, being disciplined, and learning to navigate the waves of the market. By committing to education, setting aside the right resources, and being strategic in your approach, you can tip the odds in your favor. It may be risky, but with these measures in place, you stand a far better chance of riding the highs while weathering the lows.

From Rags to Riches: Inspiring Trading Success Stories

Trading feels like navigating a stormy sea, but a midst the challenges, there are stories of traders who have sailed through turbulent waters to find success. These stories are more than tales of overnight riches; they're about persistence, learning from failure, and finding a strategy that works. Let's dive into the journeys of some traders who have gone from humble beginnings to financial success and faced the same obstacles you're grappling with now.

Small Beginnings: From $12,000 to Millions

Timothy Sykes turned $12,000 of bar mitzvah money into over $1.6 million before graduating college. His story is a classic example of how careful, calculated trading can lead to life-changing financial success. But here's the thing: it wasn't just luck. He spent countless hours researching and analyzing penny stocks before making his moves. Think of his journey as building a skyscraper—you start with a solid foundation of knowledge, layer by layer until you're at the top.

The Patient Plodder Approach

Another inspiring story is that of Ross Cameron, a trader who emphasizes the value of patience in a field that often demands quick decision-making. Cameron started with a humble account and learned the hard way—through losses, trial, and error—how to spot patterns that would eventually lead to profitable trades. His journey is like planting a garden: You don't see immediate results, but you'll reap the rewards over time with patience and consistency. He didn't hit home runs right away but built his success incrementally.

The Phoenix Rising: Coming Back From Failure

It's easy to look at successful traders and assume they've never faced setbacks. Take the story of Steven Dux, a trader who lost $50,000 in the early stages of his career. Rather than walking away, he treated this as a valuable (albeit expensive) lesson. He refined his strategies, studied the markets more thoroughly, and made a comeback, eventually turning his losses into millions in profits. Dux's story proves that failure isn't final—it's part of the learning curve.

The Corporate Quitter: From the Cubicle to the Trading Desk

Another standout story is Kunal Desai, who worked a corporate job before discovering day trading. He started small, experimenting with strategies while still working. Slowly, he built enough confidence—and financial stability—to leave his job and become a full-time trader. His path shows that success in day trading doesn't always require a dramatic leap; you can ease into it, like dipping your toes into the water before diving in.

Turning Passion Into Profit

Last but not least, is the story of Andrew Aziz, a former scientist who was laid off and decided to pursue trading full-time. He took an analytical approach to the market, applying the same scientific rigor to trading as he did to his previous career. His systematic approach paid off. Today, he's a highly successful trader who shares his strategies with others. His story highlights that day trading rewards those who bring discipline and structure to their work.

What Can We Learn From These Stories?

1. Start Small, Dream Big
2. Education Is Key
3. Patience Pays Off
4. Learn From Losses
5. Be Disciplined and Consistent

Keep learning, stay disciplined, and who knows, your story might be the next one that inspires future traders (Real, 2024).

Now that you've explored whether day trading aligns with your goals and lifestyle, let's dive into the essential knowledge and strategies you'll need before starting.

TWO

Before You Get Started

THE FUTURE BELONGS TO THOSE WHO PREPARE FOR IT TODAY. -MALCOLM X

Goals for Novice Traders: A Road map to Success

Setting clear goals is essential—think of them as your compass, guiding you through the market's choppy waters. Whether you aim to make a small profit daily or avoid significant losses, having defined goals keeps you grounded, realistic, and focused.

Why Set Goals?

Setting goals isn't just about scribbling numbers in a notebook; it's about building a framework for how you'll navigate the complexities of trading. Imagine trying to sail across the ocean without a map—you'd probably end up going in circles! Similarly, in trading, not having a plan means you're more likely to chase after short-term thrills (which often lead to losses) rather than sticking to a well-thought-out strategy.

Having realistic goals in place helps you with the following.

- **Stay disciplined:** Goals keep you focused on the bigger picture, ensuring you don't act on impulse.
- **Measure success:** Clear benchmarks let you track your progress and make the necessary changes.
- **Minimize risks:** If you set goals around risk management, you'll avoid biting off more than you can chew.

Goals Worth Setting

What kind of goals should you be setting? Here are a few examples (*How to Set Realistic Trading Goals for Your Trading Account*, 2023):

1. **Risk control:** Risk is part of the game, and controlling it is essential. Set a daily or weekly limit on how much you're willing to lose. It's like setting

up guardrails on a mountain pass—you'll still get to the top without flying off the cliff.

2. **Effort-to-reward ratio:** It's important to know what kind of return you expect for the effort you're putting in. Are you trading for multiple hours daily and only earning tiny profits, or are you managing your time wisely? Aim for a balance that doesn't leave you tired but keeps the gains coming.
3. **Profit goals:** Many traders set daily or weekly profit targets, but it's important to be realistic. Trying to hit a "home run" with every trade is like swinging for the fences and striking out more often than not. Focus on gradual growth.
4. **Reviewing trades:** An important yet often overlooked goal is setting time aside to review your trades. This is like the instant replay in sports—you get to go back and see what worked and, more importantly, what didn't. This helps refine your strategy.

How to Set and Track Trading Goals

Where do you start? Here's a simple plan (*How Do You Set and Track Trading Goals?*, 2023):

- **Be specific:** Don't just say, "I want to make more money." Try something like, "I want to achieve a 2% gain on my trading account over the next month."
- **Break it down:** It's easy to get overwhelmed by big goals. Break them down into smaller ones. For example, if your goal for the month is a profit of 2%, aim to earn 0.5% of profit per week.

- **Track your progress:** Keep a journal or use software to track every trade you make. This will give you insights into your strengths and weaknesses, allowing you to refine your goals over time.
- **Adjust as needed:** The market is ever-changing, so your goals should be flexible. Be prepared to adjust based on market conditions. If you're struggling, maybe your profit target is too aggressive—there's no shame in tweaking it.
- **Stay patient:** Rome wasn't built in a day, and neither are successful trading careers. Set long-term goals alongside your short-term ones so you stay motivated even when the daily grind feels like a chore.

Realistic vs. Unrealistic Goals

A good rule of thumb is to aim for goals that stretch you but are still within reach. For example, when training for a marathon, start by running a mile and then work your way up. Setting too lofty goals could lead to frustration and emotional decision-making, which are your worst enemies.

- **Realistic:** "I want to increase my account size by 10% over the next six months."
- **Unrealistic:** "I'm going to quit my job and trade full-time within a month."

The key is balance, which is challenging but achievable.

Build a Trading Plan

On a road trip, you wouldn't just hop in your car and drive without knowing where you're headed, right? You'd check the map, set a destination, calculate the distance, and pack everything you need. Trading is similar. You can't just dive into the markets and expect to reach your goals. A plan is your road map to success. It's a detailed guide that helps you navigate the unpredictable trading world.

Let's buckle up and break down how to create your plan—step by step.

A trading plan is a set of rules and guidelines that tell you when, why, and how to trade. It's a personal playbook that helps you make smarter decisions, manage risk, and avoid getting lost in the noise.

Think of it as a recipe. Just as you wouldn't bake a cake by randomly throwing ingredients into a bowl, you shouldn't approach trading without knowing what you're doing (Fuller, 2018).

Why Do You Need One?

Making Logical Decisions

Without a plan, your decisions are driven by emotion—fear, greed, or the dreaded FOMO (fear of missing out). A well-crafted plan lets you approach the market clearly, ensuring every trade is based on logic, not emotion.

Enhancing Discipline

A plan keeps you disciplined, like a fitness routine helps you achieve your health goals. It ensures you don't stray when things get tough. When the markets are volatile, your plan will guide your every move, like a personal financial trainer.

Easing Trading

Having a solid plan means more clarity. Imagine showing up at the gym with no idea what exercises to do. You'd wander around aimlessly, wasting time. A plan works the same way —it simplifies your routine, helping you focus on what matters.

Making Improvements

Once you've established a plan, you can tweak and improve it over time, like perfecting a recipe. You'll determine which strategies work best for you and refine them until you achieve the desired consistency.

Avoiding Huge Losses

It's no secret that trading is risky. A plan helps manage that risk by limiting how much you're willing to lose, like setting a speed limit for your road trip prevents you from speeding off a cliff.

Enjoying Trading

Believe it or not, a trading plan can make trading more enjoyable. When you have a clear structure and goals, trading feels less like gambling and more like a game you're learning to master, and who doesn't love mastering a game?

Steps to Creating a Plan

Outline Your Motivation

Why do you want to trade? It could be to make extra income, save for retirement, or because you love the thrill of the markets. Understanding your "why" keeps you motivated when the going gets tough. It's like having a playlist for your road trip that keeps you energized and focused on the journey ahead.

Decide How Much Time You Can Commit to Trading

Day trading isn't a "set it and forget it" activity. You'll need to invest time in monitoring the markets, making trades, and adjusting your strategies. Some traders treat it like a full-time job, while others only have a few hours daily. Knowing how much time you can commit to it will shape the type of plan you make.

Think of this as deciding how long you can drive in a day before pulling over to rest. Too much driving, and you'll burn out; too little, and you won't get very far.

Define Your Goals

What do you want to achieve? Are you looking for quick profits, or are you in it for the long haul? Setting clear, achievable goals, both short- and long-term, is important. It's like choosing a destination for your road trip. Are you heading to the beach for a weekend or a cross-country adventure?

Choose a Risk-Reward Ratio

Every trade you make carries risk but also offers potential rewards. You must decide how much risk you're willing to take for each reward. A common ratio is 1:3, meaning you aim to make three for every dollar you risk. This ensures that even if you lose some trades (which you will), your winning trades will more than make up for them.

When you set the stakes for a poker game, how much are you willing to bet in exchange for a shot at the big pot?

Assess Your Market Knowledge

Before diving in, take stock of how well you understand the market. Different markets (stocks, forex, and crypto) behave differently and require different strategies. Be honest with yourself. If your market knowledge is limited, set aside some time to learn more about the market (*How to Create a Successful Trading Plan*, n.d.).

Entry and Exit Rules: Knowing When to Step in and Out

At a dance party, you can't just run onto the floor whenever a random song starts, and you definitely shouldn't stay out there all night—no one wants to be the person who never leaves the dance floor. Trading is the same. Knowing when to step in (entry) and step out (exit) is important if you want to be a smooth operator.

The Rules

Entry and exit rules are like your GPS. They tell you when to jump into a trade and when to make a graceful exit. The goal is to enter a trade at just the right time—before the price starts to climb—and exit at a sweet spot, locking in your profits before the market turns against you.

These rules steer you away from emotional decision-making toward making logical moves (*Strategy Entry and Exit Rules*, 2024).

Key Elements to Include

Initial Stop Loss and Profit Target

Think of this as setting your boundaries before you even start dancing. Your initial stop loss is the point at which you're willing to say, "Okay, I've had enough. Time to leave before I embarrass myself." In trading terms, this is the price level where, if the market moves against you, you automatically exit the trade to limit your losses (Teo, 2019; Pipslow, 2023).

On the flip side, your profit target is the goal you set for yourself—when the trade reaches a certain level of profitability, it's time to cash in. It's like deciding, "I'll leave the dance floor after three songs," no matter how good the DJ is. This keeps you from getting greedy and risking your gains.

Trailing Stop

A trailing stop is like a dance partner who knows how to guide you smoothly off the floor when things start getting out of control. It's a dynamic rule that moves your stop loss toward a profitable trade as the price rises. If the market turns, the trailing stop kicks in and closes your position, locking in your profits.

For instance, if you set a trailing stop of 5% and the stock price goes up by 10%, your trailing stop will move up, ensuring you exit the trade if the price drops by more than 5% from its new high. It's like keeping an eye on the exits even while you're still enjoying the dance.

Time Stop

If you've ever stayed too long at a party and thought, "I should've left an hour ago," you'll understand this. A time stop is a rule that tells you to exit a trade if it hasn't moved as expected within a set amount of time. It's useful for day traders who don't want to leave a position open overnight or for longer than a few hours.

For instance, if you enter a trade expecting the price to rise within an hour but nothing's happened, your time stop will kick in and get you out of the trade. This prevents you from sitting in a trade going nowhere, like staying on a dance floor when the music's terrible.

Dynamic Profit Targets

This is where you keep things flexible. Dynamic profit targets adjust based on how the market is moving. Instead of having a fixed profit target (like leaving the dance after exactly three songs), you watch the market's behavior and adjust your exit accordingly.

For example, if the market is moving in your favor quickly and with high momentum, you might consider extending your profit target. It's like staying for one extra song because the DJ just started playing your favorite song. But be careful, as this strategy demands sharp attention to market signals so you don't stay too long and lose profits.

Market Exit

Sometimes, you need to leave the party when the vibe changes, whether you've hit your target or not. A market exit rule is your plan for leaving the trade even if you haven't hit your profit target yet when external factors suggest that the market's trend is reversing.

This could be triggered by sudden news, economic reports, or a market-wide trend reversal. In other words, it's like deciding to leave the dance party early because you just realized everyone's heading home (Pipslow, 2023).

Before You Place a Trade

Before diving in, you need to take a moment to assess whether you're ready.

Let's explore why self-assessment is important and ask ourselves key questions to determine whether we're prepared to place our first trades.

Jumping into trading without a self-assessment is like going on that road trip without a map or a plan—you could get lucky, but you're more likely to end up stranded. Trading isn't just about clicking buy and sell; it's about being mentally, emotionally, and strategically prepared to handle the ups and downs of the market.

Assessing yourself first lets you set the foundation for intelligent decision-making and long-term success. Let's be honest; the market is no place to wing it.

Before you place a trade, pause and ask yourself the following questions. They'll give you a solid understanding of your readiness and help you avoid unnecessary mistakes down the line.

Do I Know My Risk Tolerance?

Trading is like riding a roller coaster. Some people love the thrill, while others hold on for dear life, regretting every second. It is a wild ride, so knowing how much risk you're comfortable taking is essential. Are you okay with losing a little bit of money for the chance to win big, or do you prefer slow and steady gains?

Knowing your risk tolerance will help you formulate your strategy. Make sure it aligns with your personality and financial goals. Trading isn't a one-size-fits-all game (Baldridge, 2023).

Do I Have a Plan?

Not having a trading plan is like walking into a casino and hoping for the best. Sure, you might win a few rounds, but you'll eventually lose if you're not playing strategically.

A plan outlines when to enter and exit trades, how much risk you're willing to take, and what markets you'll focus on. If you don't have one yet, stop, take a deep breath, and make that plan before you make your next move.

How Much Capital Can I Afford to Lose

Decide how much money you can realistically afford to lose without impacting your lifestyle. This isn't a bet on your favorite sports team; you must protect your finances. Trading with money you can't afford to lose is like betting your rent at the poker table—not smart and potentially disastrous.

Am I Emotionally Ready?

Be honest with yourself: How do you handle stress? Trading can be an emotional roller coaster. One minute, you're on top of the world and the next you're watching your positions tank. If you're prone to panic, day trading could quickly become a nightmare.

Emotional control is critical to making rational decisions. If you find yourself getting anxious or overly excited when looking at market charts, it might be worth working on your emotional stability before diving in.

Is My Goal Clear?

What's the point of trading for you? Is it to make a little extra side income, or are you hoping to become a full-time trader? Defining your goals helps guide your strategy. Without a clear goal, you're like a ship without a compass—floating around without direction.

How Will I Track My Trades?

Successful traders keep detailed records of their trades to learn from their successes and mistakes. If you don't have a system in place to track what's working and what's not, you won't be able to improve. It's like cooking without tasting the food—how will you know what adjustments to make?

A simple journal helps. Write down every trade, why you made it, the outcome, and what you learned. Trust me, your future self will thank you.

Am I Prepared to Stick to My Strategy?

Sticking to a strategy is harder than it sounds, especially when the market starts acting unexpectedly. It's easy to abandon your plan in a moment of panic, but consistency is key. Ask yourself if you're disciplined enough to stick to your strategy even when making an impulsive move seems tempting.

It's like starting a diet: Cheat meals are inevitable, but don't be surprised when you don't reach your goal because you're constantly indulging.

Do I Have the Time to Commit?

Do you have the time to watch the market closely, analyze trends, and adjust your positions? If you're squeezing trades into your coffee breaks at work, it might not be the best time to jump in.

Like nurturing a plant, your trades need regular attention to grow.

How Much Do I Know About the Market?

Jumping in without understanding the market is like playing a board game without learning the rules. The more you know about how markets move, how different news affects prices, and how to analyze charts, the better your chances of success. If you're not confident in your market knowledge yet, consider spending some time learning before you risk your money.

Am I Willing to Learn From My Mistakes?

The truth is you will make mistakes. Every trader does. What distinguishes successful traders is their ability to learn from those mistakes. You're on the right track if you can bounce back, analyze what went wrong, and make improvements.

Like a puzzle, the pieces may not fit right away, but with patience and practice, you'll start seeing the bigger picture.

You Must Have an Edge

You need a competitive advantage or a "trading edge." It's like being the star player on a sports team. Without it, you're just another player in a massive game where your success hinges on skill, strategy, and perhaps a little luck. Let's break down what it means to have a trading edge, why it's essential, and how you can go about developing one to improve your odds of success.

Your trading edge is your secret weapon. It should be a unique approach or insight that helps you consistently make profitable trades. A trading edge gives you a slight advantage over the average trader. It might come from having a deep understanding of specific market trends, knowing a particular sector inside and out, or simply mastering a technical indicator.

Why Do You Need One?

Picture two chefs: One meticulously selects the best ingredients, uses precise cooking methods, and plates each dish to perfection, while the other throws ingredients together without much thought. Which chef is more likely to have satisfied customers? In trading, having an edge means you're not leaving your success to chance. It reduces the likelihood of random losses and, over time, increases your profitability (*What Is Trading Edge and Why Its Important for a Trader?*, 2023).

Examples of Trading Edges

- **Unique market insights:** Recognizing patterns, like seasonal industry trends, that others might overlook.
- **Proprietary indicators:** Custom or a specific combination of public ones (e.g., RSI with moving averages) that consistently provide reliable signals.
- **Niche knowledge:** Expertise in a specific sector (e.g., tech stocks or commodities) can help you anticipate market reactions and trends.
- **Risk management techniques:** Include stop losses or diversifying trades that protect against significant downturns.

Steps for Identifying and Developing a Trading Edge

1. **Educate yourself in the ways of the market:** Knowing the fundamentals is like learning the rules of a game. Understanding market behavior, common strategies, and economic factors gives you the foundation to build a sustainable edge.
2. **Develop your strategy:** Just as a chef might experiment with recipes before finding their signature dish, traders must try different strategies. Will you focus on technical analysis, or are you more interested in fundamental analysis? Find what aligns best with your goals.
3. **Test your strategy:** Before going all in, test your strategy with historical data to see how it would have performed. Many traders call this "back testing," which simulates your strategy's performance over time without real money on the line.
4. **Refine your strategy:** Your first strategy will rarely work perfectly. Adjust and fine-tune it based on your findings, removing what doesn't work and focusing on what does.
5. **Manage your risk:** Good traders know *when to hold 'em and when to fold 'em*. Effective risk management keeps you in the game longer, enabling you to ride out rough patches without devastating losses.
6. **Understand trading psychology:** Trading isn't just about numbers; it's also about controlling your reactions to the ups and downs of the market. A strong understanding of trading psychology—like managing fear, greed, and stress—is crucial for consistent success.

7. **Keep a trading journal:** Documenting trades lets you identify patterns and mistakes. A journal becomes your blueprint for what works and doesn't, guiding your continuous improvement.
8. **Calculate your trading edge:** This step involves analyzing your win/loss ratio and average returns to determine if your edge gives you a positive expected outcome. Think of it like checking your grades after every semester: Are you meeting your goals?
9. **Be patient, rinse, and repeat:** Building an edge isn't a one-time activity. Re-evaluate and adjust as the market evolves. Remember, patience is vital; consistent effort yields the best results over time.

Simulated Trading

Before trading, consider practicing with simulated (or paper) trading. It's like trying a recipe in a test kitchen before opening a restaurant: You can perfect your craft without fearing financial loss.

Benefits of Paper Trading

- **Risk-free learning:** Since no real money is involved, you can learn from your mistakes without financial consequences.
- **Confidence building:** The more you practice, the more comfortable you'll feel when it's time to trade with real funds.
- **Strategy testing:** Experiment with different approaches and strategies to find what works best for you (Bajpai, 2024).

Downsides of Paper Trading

- **Lack of real-world pressure:** Real-money trading brings a different level of psychological pressure, which paper trading doesn't replicate.
- **False confidence:** Winning trades on paper may not translate to success with real money because emotional factors are absent from simulations.

Establishing Emergency Funds

An emergency fund is your financial safety net. Like a spare tire for your car, it's there when you need it most, allowing you to continue your journey without major setbacks.

Reasons to Have an Emergency Fund

1. **Margin calls:** If a trade turns against you, your broker may demand additional funds to cover potential losses.
2. **Unforeseen losses:** Markets can be unpredictable, so an emergency fund helps you manage unanticipated dips.
3. **Avoid impulse decisions:** Knowing you have a financial cushion allows you to stick to your strategy without the temptation of making impulsive moves.
4. **Market Volatility:** Protects against drastic changes that could wipe out smaller accounts.
5. **Reduce stress and anxiety:** Knowing you're financially prepared can ease the emotional toll of trading.

6. **Opportunity capitalization:** An emergency fund allows you to seize unplanned opportunities without jeopardizing your core capital.

How Much to Set Aside as an Emergency Fund

Set aside at least 3–6 months of your trading capital. This ensures that you're well-prepared for any disruptions.

How to Build an Emergency Fund

- **Set a goal:** Determine how much you want in your fund, aiming for the 3–6-month range as a minimum.
- **Make regular contributions:** Dedicate a portion of your profits to the fund until you reach your goal.
- **Keep it separate:** Keep your emergency fund in a separate account, away from your active trading funds.

When you understand these essentials—your edge, practicing with simulated trading, and securing an emergency fund, you'll set a strong foundation that can improve your odds and give you peace of mind in the high-stakes trading world.

With your foundational knowledge in place, it's time to step inside the trading room and set up the tools you'll rely on daily.

THREE

Inside the Trading Room

Don't worry about what the markets are going to do; worry about what you will do in response to the markets.

Michael Carr

Trading Room Setup

Imagine yourself as a pilot with your trading room as the cockpit. Every tool, piece of hardware, and connection must be up to speed to ensure a smooth, successful flight. Whether you're a novice or a seasoned pro looking to up your game, the way you set up your trading room makes all the difference. Let's dive into the essentials, starting with the most important equipment: your computer setup.

Computer Setup

Your computer is your engine. Just like you wouldn't drive a car with a lawnmower engine, you shouldn't skimp on your computer hardware to navigate the high-speed trading world. Let's break down the components needed to build a high-performing, lightning-fast trading machine.

The Processor

The processor is similar to your brain's decision-making center—only faster if you pick the right one. You'll need a central processing unit or CPU that can quickly handle large amounts of data, allowing you to make split-second decisions. Look for multi-core processors like Intel i7 or AMD Ryzen 7, as they can juggle multiple tasks without breaking a sweat. If you go for lower specs, you'll end up like a sprinter wearing flip-flops—slow and ineffective.

Hard Drive

Speed is the name of the game. Opt for a solid-state drive (SSD) over a traditional hard disk drive (HDD). Why? Imagine trying to access your data as fast as grabbing a book off the shelf (SSD) versus sifting through a dusty old library (HDD). SSDs offer quicker boot-up times, faster software launches, and less downtime on trading days. Think of it as your fast-track ticket to staying ahead in the game.

Graphics Card

While day trading doesn't demand the same graphical power as gaming or design work, a solid graphics processing unit or GPU will help ensure that your charts and trading platforms run smoothly. A dedicated graphics card, like an NVIDIA GTX 1050 or higher, can handle multiple monitors and large data streams. Without it, you'll feel like you're driving a Ferrari but stuck in first gear.

Monitor(s)

Day traders often use multiple monitors to monitor charts, news feeds, and trades simultaneously. Ideally, aim for at least two or three 24-inch monitors. You'll feel surrounded by a control tower, with each monitor representing a different aspect of your strategy. Make sure your setup is ergonomic by using monitor racks to adjust the height and position comfortably.

Adapters

Let's not forget the unsung heroes of your setup: the USB and HDMI adapters. These tiny gadgets ensure that all your devices are connected. Trading platforms, software, and monitors all need to work together. Just like a chef relies on every utensil, you'll need all the right connections to keep your system running efficiently.

Here Is Why You Need High-Speed Internet

Once your computer is set up and ready to go, you'll need one more key ingredient: high-speed internet. Imagine trying to make a trade with the same speed as dial-up! Not only would you be left behind, but you could also miss out on profitable opportunities. Let's examine why having a fast, reliable internet is essential for traders (*Why Stock Traders Need Fast Internet*, 2022).

Efficient Collaboration

Trading isn't a solo venture. You'll need to collaborate with brokers, access real-time data, and engage in forums or platforms where you share ideas with other traders. A laggy connection can disrupt this. A good analogy is trying to have a conversation underwater—everything sounds muffled and slow. High-speed internet makes communication seamless, just like chatting in person.

Reliable Services

Trading platforms, charting software, and news feeds all rely on a steady stream of data. If your internet isn't up to par, you'll experience lags or, worse, disconnections during an important trade. It's like trying to run a marathon and tripping over every stone. High-speed internet ensures that your trading tools remain reliable, allowing you to stay on top of market movements.

Secure Network

In the digital world, security is paramount. Slow internet connections can make your network more vulnerable to cyber-attacks, potentially compromising sensitive financial information. A secure, high-speed connection is like a sturdy lock on your digital front door, keeping hackers and malware at bay. You wouldn't leave your wallet on a park bench—don't leave your network exposed either.

Minimum Internet Parameters to Consider for Stock Trading

You don't want to settle for *okay* internet speed. Here's a quick breakdown of the minimum requirements you should meet for optimal trading performance:

- **Internet bandwidth:** At least 40 Mbps. This is your internet's capacity to handle data. It's like the size of a pipe—the bigger the pipe, the more data can flow through at once. Anything less than 40 Mbps risks a bottleneck in your trades.
- **Network latency:** At most 5 milliseconds. This measures the delay between when you send data and when it's received. High latency is like talking to someone through a tin can phone—by the time you finish speaking, the moment is gone. Keep latency low for quick, responsive trading.
- **Packet loss:** Zero percent. No excuses here. Packet loss is like sending a message, but some words disappear along the way. Even the most minor data loss could mean the difference between profit and loss in trading.

Ways to Improve Internet Speed

Sometimes, traffic jams happen, slowing everything down, and that's when you miss out on those critical opportunities. The good news is you can boost your internet speed with a few tweaks, and most of them are easy to make. Let's discuss some easy yet effective strategies to improve your connection (Parrish, 2022).

Restart Your Router or Internet Gateway (Modem/Router Combo)

Like a coffee machine, your router works great at first, but after a while, it gets sluggish if you don't give it a break. The easiest fix? Turn it off and back on. Restarting your router gives it a fresh start, clearing any clogs in your connection. It's like giving your tired coffee machine a clean filter so it starts working like new.

Move Your Router to a Better Spot

Your router may be shy, hiding in the corner of your room, but it needs a central stage. The more open space around your router, the better the signal will travel. If your router is hiding in a closet or behind a bookshelf, it's like trying to shout instructions to someone from another room—the message will get misinterpreted. Move it to a central, elevated spot for maximum reach.

Use 5 GHz Wi-Fi Over 2.4 GHz Wi-Fi

Wi-Fi bands are like roadways. On the one hand, the 2.4 GHz band is like a two-lane country road—it gets crowded easily and moves slowly. On the other hand, 5 GHz Wi-Fi is like a wide, multi-lane freeway with fewer cars and faster speeds. If your device supports it, switch to 5 GHz for less congestion and quicker data flow. The only downside? The freeway doesn't stretch as far, so you might lose the signal if you're too far away.

Adjust Your Router Antennas

Routers broadcast signals in all directions. If your router has antennas, make sure they're adequately angled. Pointing them in different directions—vertically and horizontally—can help the signal cover more ground. It's like adjusting a sprinkler to water your entire garden, not just one patch of grass. Your Wi-Fi signal will reach more areas of your home or office.

Add a Wi-Fi Extender for More Range

If your internet still struggles to reach certain areas of your home, try a Wi-Fi extender. A Wi-Fi extender picks up your existing signal and carries it further so you can browse the web (or make trades) from the comfort of any room. It's like having a friend who relays your message across the house—no more shouting, just smooth, extended coverage.

Remove Unnecessary Devices

Have you ever noticed how a crowded restaurant slows down service? The same goes for your internet connection. The more devices connected to your Wi-Fi, the slower everything becomes. Do you need your smart fridge to be online while you're trading? Consider disconnecting devices that aren't in use. Freeing up bandwidth is akin to clearing out a busy pub so the bartender can focus on your tab—you'll get quicker, more responsive service.

Switch to a Less Crowded Wi-Fi Channel

Wi-Fi channels are like radio frequencies. Sometimes, your router and your neighbors' routers jam the same signal, causing interference. Switching to a less crowded Wi-Fi channel is like changing the radio station to one with fewer listeners—you'll get a clearer, faster connection. Most routers have a built-in feature to pick the best channel automatically or you can manually choose one in your router's settings.

Upgrade Your Internet Plan

If you've tried everything else and your internet still feels slower than a turtle on roller skates, it might be time to look at your internet plan. Sometimes, the solution is upgrading to a higher-speed package. Think of it as upgrading from roller skates to a bicycle—suddenly, everything moves faster and smoother. It may cost a bit more, but the increase in speed could pay off when those trades start landing in real-time (Gilbertson, 2024).

Buying Long, Selling Short

Imagine the stock market as a giant buffet. You can fill your plate with as much as you want (buying long) or spot something you don't like and bet others won't like it (selling short). These are the two main strategies traders use. While polar opposites, they are both part of a balanced trading diet. Let's dig in and understand the critical differences between them.

Buying Long: The Classic

When you take a long position, you're essentially saying, "I believe this stock is going to go up, and I want in on the action!" It's like buying a cake at the buffet because you think more people will want it later. You hold onto your slice, expecting its value to rise, and then sell it to someone else for a profit when demand peaks.

- **How it works:** You purchase a stock, hoping its price will increase. If it does, you sell it for a profit. If it doesn't, you can hold on or sell at a loss, depending on your strategy.
- **Why it's popular:** Buying long is a straightforward way to profit from the stock market. You're betting on a company's growth, and as long as you're patient, you may benefit from long-term price increases.

- **Risk factor:** Your losses are limited to the amount you invested, and while waiting for the stock price to rise, you may earn dividends (depending on the stock). It's like holding onto that slice of cake even if it goes stale because you'll never lose more than what you paid for it.

Selling Short: Betting on the Downside

Let's flip the script. Here, you're betting that a stock's price will fall. Imagine you see a cake at the buffet, but instead of buying it, you borrow it from the chef and sell it to another diner at its current price. You hope that after everyone has had a taste, demand will drop, and you can buy back the cake from someone else at a lower price, return it to the chef, and pocket the difference.

- **How it works:** In short selling, you borrow shares of a stock and sell them at the current price. You hope the stock's value will decrease so you can buy the shares back at a lower price and return them, keeping the difference as profit.
- **Why traders love it:** Short selling lets traders profit when the market goes down. It's a popular strategy when stocks are expected to decline, allowing traders to benefit from market downturns.
- **Risk factor:** Unlike buying long, short selling carries higher risk. If the stock price rises instead, your losses can be theoretically infinite. It's like betting that no one will want the cake anymore, only to find out it's suddenly a hit dessert. Now you have to buy

back that cake at an inflated price, and there's no limit to how much it might cost.

Key Differences Between Long and Short Positions

- **Direction of profit**: In a long position, you're betting on rising prices. In a short position, you're betting on prices going down.
- **Risk exposure:** When buying long, your maximum loss is the amount you invested. When selling short, losses can be unlimited if stock prices skyrocket.
- **Mindset:** Long traders are optimistic—they believe the market will go up. Short sellers are pessimists or opportunists looking to profit from market declines.

Buying long is like walking into the stock market with rose-colored glasses, expecting good things while selling short is for the realist (or cynic) who bets that things will go wrong.

High-Frequency Trading

High-frequency trading (HFT) is the Formula 1 of the stock market. It's all about speed. HFT traders use complex algorithms and super-fast computers to make thousands of trades in the blink of an eye. Think of them as race car drivers zooming through the stock market, looking to make profits from the tiniest price changes. However, like any race, advantages and risks are involved (Chen, 2021).

What Is HFT?

HFT refers to using powerful computers and algorithms to execute a high volume of trades at lightning speed. These trades happen so fast that a regular human trader wouldn't be able to keep up.

How Does it Work?

HFT firms place their computers physically close to stock exchanges (in the same building!) to reduce latency, which is the time it takes for information to travel. Their algorithms can detect minuscule price differences between markets or anticipate short-term trends, allowing them to make profitable trades before the rest of the market catches up.

Advantages

- **Speed:** HFT allows firms to execute trades within microseconds, taking advantage of price discrepancies or fleeting market inefficiencies.
- **Liquidity:** By making so many trades, HFT firms add liquidity to the market, making it easier for other traders to buy and sell stocks.
- **Profit potential:** Since HFT strategies rely on speed and volume, traders can make small but consistent profits that add up over time.

Risks

- **Market manipulation:** HFT has been criticized for creating unfair advantages. By acting so quickly, these firms can manipulate stock prices, often before other traders have had a chance to react.

- **Flash crashes:** The speed and volume of HFT can lead to market instability, contributing to sudden drops or *flash crashes* where prices plummet within seconds.
- **Cost:** Running an HFT operation isn't cheap. The technology and infrastructure needed to compete in this space can be prohibitively expensive for smaller players.

HFT is like having a supercharged car on the stock market's racetrack. You'll get to the finish line faster, but the risks of crashing are also much higher.

Institutional Traders vs. Retail Traders: What's the Difference?

They are like the David and Goliath of the market. If the stock market were a playground, institutional traders would be the cool kids with all the best gear, while retail traders would be the scrappy underdogs with a lot of heart. But what's the real difference between the two, and why does it matter?

Institutional Traders: The Big Players

They work for large firms like banks, hedge funds, and pension funds. They manage vast sums of money and have access to sophisticated tools and information. It's like being the kid with the brand-new bike and the best sneakers—you can dominate the playground when you've got the gear.

Advantages

- Access to massive resources and research teams.
- They can influence market prices because of the size of their trades.
- Often have lower trading costs due to high volumes.

Disadvantages

- Under constant scrutiny from regulators.
- They can sometimes move the market in unintended ways, which makes them less agile.

Retail Traders: The Everyday Investors

They are individuals who buy and sell stocks through their personal accounts. They may not have access to the same resources as institutional traders, but they have the flexibility to act quickly and make decisions without corporate red tape. Think of them as the kid who knows how to turn a stick and some string into a winning kite—they may not have fancy tools, but they make the most of what they've got.

Advantages

- Flexibility to make quick decisions without institutional constraints.
- Can take on smaller, niche positions that aren't available to big players.
- Higher trading costs per trade, but the freedom to act quickly is a significant advantage.

Disadvantages

- Lack of access to the same information and technology as institutional traders.
- Higher fees and less buying power compared to institutions.

Ultimately, both have their place in the market, each with unique strengths and weaknesses. Whether you're riding with the big dogs or flying solo, it's important to know your strengths and play to them (Palmer, 2022).

With your trading setup ready, let's explore the mindset and emotional resilience you'll need to navigate the market's ups and downs.

FOUR

On the Safer Side

You can never protect yourself 100%. What you do is protect yourself as much as possible and mitigate risk to an acceptable degree. You can never remove all risk.

Kevin Mitnick

Trading Psychology Explained: Mastering Your Emotions for Success

Have you heard the saying, "The market is 90% emotion and 10% logic?" While it's a bit of an exaggeration, it's not far from the truth. Trading psychology, or how you feel and behave while making trades, is crucial to your success. Think of the stock market as a roller coaster with exhilarating highs and terrifying lows. It's easy to get swept up in the thrill of it all, but to succeed, you need to stay grounded. Let's break down why your mindset matters and how you can develop the mental fortitude of a seasoned trader.

Handling Emotions: Keeping Your Cool in the Market

Trading is an emotional game. Imagine you're a quarterback in the final seconds of a tied game—you wouldn't make the winning pass if you were panicking. Similarly, your emotions can make or break your trades. Managing them, no matter the outcome, is a skill every trader needs to develop.

Why It Matters

Imagine you're in a trade, and the market starts to tank. You'll feel fear. What would you do? Without emotional control, you might hit that "sell" button too soon and lock in a loss. Or maybe greed takes over after a win, and you keep pushing your luck, hoping for more. Both scenarios lead to poor decision-making and, ultimately, losses.

Common Emotions Traders Experience

Let's break down these common emotions and how they can influence behavior:

- **Fear:** It makes you second-guess yourself and often leads to premature decisions.
- **Conviction:** Being firm in your analysis is essential, but overconfidence can close your eyes to red flags.
- **Greed:** Ah, the downfall of many. Greed whispers, "Just one more trade, and I'll make a fortune." But chasing more can lead to reckless trades.

The Consequences of Letting Emotions Rule Your Trades

Imagine driving a car without paying attention to road signs. Emotions have the same effect when you trade. Here are some ways unchecked emotions can derail your success:

- **Following the herd:** When the market moves in a frenzy, it's tempting to follow the crowd. But just because everyone else is jumping off a cliff doesn't mean you should.
- **FOMO:** You see a stock rising fast and feel the urge to jump in. However, without research, this impulse can lead to buying high and selling low.
- **Ignoring stop loss:** You've set your stop-loss order, but as the price drops, you convince yourself it will recover. Ignoring your stop loss is like removing your seat belt during a crash.
- **Impulsive trading:** When your emotions dictate your trades, you're no longer following a plan but reacting. Impulsive trades usually end in regret.

- **Chasing losses:** After a losing trade, you might feel compelled to recover your losses by making another trade immediately. This can snowball into even more significant losses, like trying to catch a falling knife.

Tips to Control Your Emotions While Trading

Here are some strategies to help you stay in control when things get turbulent:

- **Create personal rules:** Set clear guidelines for entering and exiting trades and stick to them. Having rules helps curb emotional decision-making.
- **Lower your trade size:** If the fear of losing is overwhelming, reduce the size of your trades. Smaller trades lower the stakes, making it easier to stay calm and rational.
- **Trade in the right market conditions:** Only trade when the market aligns with your strategy. Just because the market is open doesn't mean it's the right time for you to move.

Trading is like surfing—you can't control the waves, but you can control how you ride them. Developing a strong, disciplined mindset will keep you on your board, riding the waves of the market instead of being swept away by them.

Following these tips and being mindful of how emotions influence your trades will help you think more like a pro trader and less like a nervous beginner. It's not about avoiding emotions altogether but learning to manage them so they work for and not against you (Lund, n.d.).

Develop a Trader's Mindset: Stay Sharp and Cool Under Pressure

Think of the tortoise and the hare. It's not just about running fast but pacing yourself, staying focused, and knowing when to push and when to rest. Just like an athlete needs a game plan and discipline, traders must develop a strong mindset. Here are some tips to help you cultivate the mindset of a successful trader:

Keep a Trading Log: Your Playbook

A good coach always reviews game footage. A trading log is your *highlight reel*, showing what worked and what didn't. Jotting down your trades, why you made them, and how they turned out lets you spot patterns in your good and not-so-good decisions. Over time, your log becomes a treasure trove of insights, helping you improve.

Trader Thinking: Stay in the Zone

Imagine you're a chess player, thinking two or three moves ahead. Successful traders don't just react to the market; they anticipate it. "Trader thinking" is all about strategy. Instead of focusing on the short-term noise, step back and see the bigger picture. Stay calm and avoid impulsive decisions by always considering the long game.

Develop and Follow a Trading Plan: Your GPS for the Market

Trading feels like reading a map when you don't have a plan. A solid trading plan is like having a GPS—it helps you stay on track, no matter the twists and turns. Set your goals, define your risk tolerance, and stick to your strategy. If you ever feel lost, revisit the plan.

Control Your Emotions: Keep a Cool Head

There are highs, lows, and moments that make your heart race. But if you let fear, greed, or excitement drive your decisions, you will likely make mistakes. Keep your emotions in check by setting clear rules and sticking to them, no matter how much the market tempts you to do otherwise.

Control Your Losses: Know When to Fold 'Em

Just like in poker, a good trader knows when to hold and when to fold. Losses are inevitable, but the key is to control them. Set stop-loss orders to automatically exit trades before things go too far south, and remember that no one wins 100% of the time. The goal isn't to avoid losses altogether but to minimize them.

Keep Learning: The Market Is Your Classroom

The market is constantly evolving, and so should you. Whether by reading books, taking courses, or staying updated on market trends, a successful trader always continues learning. Think of it as a never-ending adventure where each new skill or piece of knowledge brings you one step closer to mastering the market.

Patience: Play the Long Game

Rome wasn't built in a day, and neither was success. One of the most important traits of a good trader is patience. Sometimes, the best action is no action at all. Wait for the proper setup and conditions, and don't feel pressured to trade just for the sake of it (*How to Create a Successful Trading Plan*, n.d.).

Losses Are Inevitable: Accept the Bumps in the Road

Losses are part of the journey. They're like speed bumps—they slow you down but don't stop you unless you let them. The key is to learn from your losses without letting them discourage you. Every great trader has faced setbacks, but they kept moving forward.

Tips to Stay Focused

Think of self-discipline as the engine of a successful mindset. Without it, even the best strategies can fall apart. Here's how to sharpen your self-discipline and stay on course:

Direct Your Attention to What Needs to Be Done

For a race car driver, every second counts, and distractions can cost them the race. In trading, distractions (like checking social media or second-guessing your strategy) can lead to missed opportunities or poor decisions. Stay focused on what needs to be done, and don't let the noise around you derail your plan.

Drive the Negative Vibes Away

Negative thoughts can cloud your judgment. If you let fear, frustration, or doubt take over, you'll likely make rash decisions. Like an athlete shaking off a bad play, traders need to clear their heads after a losing trade. Shift your mindset back to what you can control and push forward with a positive outlook.

Keep the End in Mind: Eyes on the Prize

When the going gets tough, remind yourself why you started in the first place. Whether it's financial freedom, personal growth, or mastering a skill, keeping your long-term goal in mind helps you stay disciplined. It's like hiking up a mountain—when the climb feels hard, remember the incredible view waiting for you at the top.

Potential Risks

Trading feels like a fast-paced adventure, like racing down a hill. The thrill is undeniable, but you could hit some serious bumps along the way if you're not careful. Understanding the risks is like knowing where the potholes are. So, let's take a look at the different types of risks every trader should be aware of before going full speed.

- **Market risk:** Market risk is like weather—you can't control it, and sometimes a storm rolls in when you least expect it. This is the risk of market conditions going against you. Prices can shift due to factors like economic reports or world events. It's essential to be prepared for anything, even on what seems like a sunny day.

- **Operational risk:** Operational risk is like your bike suddenly breaking down mid-ride. It could be anything from a power outage to a software glitch that prevents you from making trades at the right moment. It's frustrating and can cost you money, but ensuring you have a solid setup with backup plans can help keep things rolling smoothly.
- **Liquidity risk:** Liquidity risk happens when you want to get out of a trade, but there's no one to sell to, almost like being stuck in traffic when you need to get somewhere fast. If a market is illiquid, it can be difficult to buy or sell quickly at a fair price, which could mean you're left holding onto a position longer than planned.
- **Counterparty risk:** Counterparty risk is the risk that the other party in your trade doesn't hold up their end of the deal, like lending your bike to someone and worrying they won't return it. When trading, especially in less regulated markets, you trust that brokers, exchanges, or other parties will settle their trades as promised. If they don't, you could face financial losses.
- **Legal risk:** Imagine biking in a race, only to find out the rules have changed halfway through. Legal risk is about the potential for new regulations or laws that could affect your trading. Staying informed about current regulations and upcoming changes helps you avoid being blindsided by unexpected restrictions or penalties.

- **Political risk:** Political risk is like a sudden roadblock that forces you to take a detour. It happens when political events, like elections or new government policies, affect market conditions. While these events may be out of your control, being aware of them can help you anticipate potential market shifts.
- **Credit risk:** Credit risk is like selling lemonade to a customer, but they run off without paying. In trading, this happens when the other party defaults on their obligation to pay or deliver the securities. It's rare but can happen, particularly in less regulated or over-the-counter markets.
- **Diversification:** "Don't put all your eggs in one basket" is diversification in a nutshell. If you invest all your money in one trade, one wrong move could break your entire basket. Spreading out your investments across different assets or markets helps you balance the risk and avoid significant losses.
- **Interconnection risk:** Interconnection risk is like a line of dominoes—when one falls, the rest could follow. In today's globalized world, markets are highly interconnected. A crisis in one country or market can spill over into others, affecting your trades even if you're not directly involved. Keeping an eye on global events can help you avoid these chain reactions.

How Much Risk Can You Tolerate?

Before jumping in, you must determine how much risk you can handle. It's like deciding whether to ride the roller coaster or stick to the merry-go-round.

What Is Risk Tolerance?

Risk tolerance is your *comfort zone regarding risks. Can you* stomach big ups and downs, or do you prefer a slower, steadier pace? Your risk tolerance determines how much fluctuation you can handle in your portfolio without losing sleep (Baldridge, 2023).

Factors That Influence Your Risk Tolerance

Everyone's risk tolerance is different, and it can be shaped by the following factors:

- **Age:** Younger traders might have a higher tolerance for risk because they have more time to recover from losses. Older traders might prefer a more conservative approach.
- **Experience:** Newbies may want to play it safe, while seasoned traders may be more willing to take on risk.
- **Financial situation:** If you depend on your trading income for daily expenses, you might want to be more cautious.
- **Personality:** Some people love the thrill of taking risks, while others feel more secure with a safety net (Schwab, 2017).

How to Determine Your Risk Tolerance

Start by asking yourself these questions:

- How much of my capital will I lose on a single trade?
- How do I handle losses—do they stress me out or motivate me to improve?
- Am I looking for slow and steady growth, or am I aiming for big wins?

Answering these questions honestly will help you determine what level of risk is right for you (*Questions to Determine Your Investment Risk Tolerance*, 2023).

The Cost of Ignoring Risk

Ignoring risk is like driving without brakes: It might work for a while, but eventually, you'll crash. Here's what could happen if you don't take risks seriously:

- **Overconfidence:** If you ignore risk, you might feel invincible, leading to reckless trades that could wipe out your capital.
- **Losses pile up:** Without proper risk management, one bad trade can turn into a series of losses that spiral out of control.
- **Missed opportunities:** Focusing too much on the upside without considering the downside means you could miss chances to cut your losses or take profits when necessary (McBride, 2024).

Risk Mitigation Strategies

Like surfing, trading is thrilling, but you must know how to ride the waves without being wiped out. Risk mitigation strategies are the tools that keep you afloat, helping you avoid significant losses and maximize gains. Let's break down these strategies in a way that's easy to follow and understand so you can confidently ride those waves (Yazdanparast, 2021).

Setting Stop-Loss Levels: Your Safety Net

Imagine a stop loss as a safety net that catches you before you fall too far. A stop-loss order automatically sells your position if it drops to a certain price, limiting your losses.

- **What's a stop loss?** A stop loss is a pre-set price that automatically triggers a sale of your assets when they fall below a certain level. Consider it your "exit button" when things aren't going your way.
- **Why use a stop loss?** It helps you avoid significant losses by cutting off a losing trade early. It's like jumping off the surfboard before the big wave crashes.

Tips for Determining Your Stop-Loss Level

Consider your risk tolerance and trading goals. Your stop loss should be neither too close (you'll get out too early) nor too far away (you'll lose more than planned).

Setting Stop Loss Like a Pro

- **Identify the market structure:** Just like a surfer reading the waves, you need to understand market trends before setting a stop loss. Look for essential support and resistance levels.
- **Set your stop loss away from the market structure:** Don't place your stop loss right at the "breakpoint." Give it some breathing room so you don't get stopped by minor fluctuations.

AI-Enhanced Stop-Loss Strategies

Using AI to enhance your stop-loss strategies is like having a surf instructor telling you when to ride and when to hold back. Here's how AI can improve your trading game:

- **Improved risk management:** AI can monitor multiple factors simultaneously, allowing you to manage risk more effectively.
- **Adaptability:** AI adjusts to changing market conditions faster than humans can.
- **Increased precision:** It places your stop loss at the most optimal points based on real-time data.
- **Time efficiency:** AI helps you make decisions faster, saving you valuable time.

Setting Take-Profit Levels

Take-profit orders are like knowing when to paddle back to shore after a great wave. It locks in your gains when the market reaches a certain price level.

- **What's a take-profit order?** When your desired profit target is reached, a take-profit order automatically sells your position.
- **Why use it?** It helps you cash out at the right time without getting greedy or emotional. But beware: Sometimes, the market can continue after your target, and you might miss out on further gains.
- **Common take-profit mistakes:** Setting your target too high or too low. Like surfing, timing is everything (Teo, 2023).

Balancing Act: Combining Stop-Loss and Take-Profit Orders

Think of stop-loss and take-profit orders as the perfect balance on your surfboard. One helps you avoid big losses, and the other locks in your gains. Using both together keeps you in control, even when the waves are unpredictable.

Position Sizing

Position sizing is like deciding how big of a surfboard you need. Too big or too small, and you'll lose balance.

- **What's position sizing?** It's the amount of money you allocate to a single trade. The goal is to balance risk and reward based on your account size.
- **Tips for optimizing position size:** Base it on your experience level, account size, and risk-reward ratio. Remember, over committing can lead to significant losses, while under committing can limit your potential returns (Chen, 2019).

Other Risk Mitigation Strategies: Safety Gear for Traders

Even the best surfers wear safety gear, and day traders need tools, too. Here are some additional strategies for minimizing risk:

- **Be mindful of leverage:** Leverage can amplify both gains and losses, so use it wisely.
- **Build a trading plan:** A well-thought-out plan keeps you on track and lessens emotional decision-making.
- **Control your risk per trade:** Never risk more than a small percentage of your total capital on a single trade.
- **Diversification:** Spread your investments across different markets.
- **Hedging:** Reduce risk by taking positions that can offset potential losses in your main trades.
- **Manage your emotions**: Trading is emotional, but letting feelings take over can lead to poor decisions. Stay calm and stick to your strategy.

Riding the Storm

Even professional traders wipe out sometimes, but they know how to get back on the board. Here's what they do:

- **Stick to their plan:** They follow their strategies without letting emotions dictate their moves.
- **Manage risk first:** They focus on protecting their capital before chasing profits.

- **Learn from mistakes:** Every loss is a lesson. Pro traders analyze what went wrong and use it to improve.

Implementing these risk mitigation strategies lets you ride the market waves with confidence, knowing that you've taken steps to protect yourself from major wipe outs.

Now that you have a grasp on the psychological side, it's time to think about the instruments. To build a well-rounded strategy, let's explore the various assets you can trade, from stocks to bonds and beyond.

FIVE

What to Trade

Choices have consequences.

Scott Sigler

Exchange-Traded Funds

Exchange-traded funds (ETFs) are a basket of assets grouped together to be traded as a single unit. Imagine buying a "sample platter" at a restaurant: Instead of ordering one item, you get a taste of several dishes, diversifying your risk across different assets. ETFs can track various assets like stocks, commodities, or even bonds, giving you the flexibility of investing in a sector or an entire index without picking individual stocks (*ETFs for Beginners*, 2023).

Features

- **Liquidity:** ETFs are highly liquid, meaning you can buy and sell them throughout the day, like stocks.
- **Diversification:** ETFs often spread their holdings across a range of assets, reducing the risk tied to any single investment.
- **Lower cost:** With lower fees than many mutual funds, ETFs are a cost-effective choice for traders looking to diversify without high management fees.

Common Strategies

- **Sector or thematic ETFs:** These ETFs focus on specific sectors, like technology or healthcare, allowing traders to capitalize on trends in that industry.

- **Leveraged and inverse ETFs:** Leveraged ETFs amplify the daily returns of an index or asset class, while inverse ETFs provide the opposite returns. Both are risky but potentially rewarding for day traders who can handle short-term swings.

Pros and Cons

Pros	Cons
Lower cost and management fees	Lower potential for high returns compared to individual stocks
Diversification reduces individual asset risk	High risk and not ideal for beginners
High liquidity and flexibility	May have tracking errors if they don't perfectly mirror their underlying assets

How to Invest

- **Choose a brokerage:** Most major brokerages offer access to ETFs. Look for one with low fees and robust trading tools.
- **Research sector-specific ETFs:** Identify ETFs in sectors you're interested in, like tech or energy.
- **Consider volume and liquidity:** Choose ETFs with high daily volume for smoother day trading.
- **Practice timing:** Watch for times of day when trading volume is high to make quick trades.

Stocks

Stocks represent ownership in individual companies and are day trading staples because of their volatility and potential for short-term gains. Investing in a stock is like betting on a horse in a race—each company's performance can differ vastly based on external and internal factors.

Features

- **Volatility:** Stock prices experience rapid price fluctuations, leading to risks and rewards.
- **Earning potential:** Stocks often provide the highest earning potential among traditional trading instruments, attracting active traders.
- **Corporate ties:** Stocks are directly influenced by a company's earnings reports, news, and overall performance.

Common Strategies

- **Scalping:** This strategy involves making multiple small trades throughout the day to profit from tiny price movements. Scalpers often exit within minutes and aim for a high volume of trades.
- **News-based trading:** Major corporate news or announcements can significantly impact stock prices. For instance, earnings reports or product launches create opportunities to trade on immediate price movements.

Pros and Cons

Pros	Cons
High earning potential	High risk due to volatility
Vast variety of options to trade	May require a high level of research
Accessible with fractional shares	Requires attention to company news and market events

How to Invest

- **Pick a reputable broker**: Choose a brokerage that offers low commissions and access to research tools and trading charts.
- **Focus on high-volume stock:** Stocks with high trading volume tend to have smaller spreads, making it easier to enter and exit trades.
- **Set realistic goals:** Stocks can be profitable but also come with risks. Start with a limited amount to gauge your comfort level.
- **Stay informed:** Use financial news, earnings calendars, and stock screeners to stay updated on stocks in your portfolio (Davis, 2024).

Indices

Indices are like a stock market highlight reel. They track the performance of a group of stocks within a specific sector or market. For instance, the S&P 500 represents 500 top U.S. companies and gives a glimpse of the overall market health. Indices are popular with day traders who prefer trading on broader market movements rather than individual companies (*What Are Indices?*, n.d.).

Features

- **Benchmark representation:** Indices serve as a barometer for specific sectors or entire markets, giving traders a view of market trends.
- **Lower volatility:** Indices tend to be less volatile than individual stocks, making them suitable for traders who want less exposure to single-company risks.
- **Limited ownership:** Unlike stocks or ETFs, you don't actually "own" part of an index but can trade contracts based on its value.

Common Strategies

Trend following: Traders analyze trends within an index, identifying patterns to predict future movements.

Mean reversion: This strategy assumes an index will return to its average level after significant deviations, providing opportunities for both buying and selling.

Pros and Cons

Pros	Cons
Reflects broader market trends	Less flexible for specific sector-focused trading
Lower volatility than individual stocks	Some indices have fewer trading options compared to stocks
Easier to analyze market-wide movements	Requires contracts rather than direct ownership

How to Invest

- **Use a broker with index access:** Choose a platform that offers index trading options, like futures or options contracts.
- **Research market news:** Major economic reports or geopolitical events can shift entire indices.
- **Time Your trades:** Indices are affected by macroeconomic data released at specific times, so strategize entry and exit points accordingly.
- **Consider ETFs tracking indices:** If direct index trading isn't available, index-tracking ETFs offer a similar exposure.

Bonds

Bonds are loans you give to a company or government in exchange for interest payments. They're often used by traders who prefer lower risk but still want steady returns. Bonds offer fixed interest payments, and their prices are frequently influenced by changes in interest rates (Carlson, 2020).

Features

- **Steady income:** Bonds pay fixed interest over time, making them ideal for consistent earnings.
- **Interest rate sensitivity:** When interest rates rise, bond prices fall, and vice versa, making bond prices predictable based on rate expectations.

- **Different types:** Bonds vary in duration and issuer. Short-term bonds are less affected by interest rates than long-term bonds.

Common Strategies

- **Interest rate speculation:** By predicting interest rate trends, traders can buy or sell bonds based on expected price changes.
- **Yield spread trading:** This involves trading on the spread between long-term and short-term bond yields to capture gains from fluctuating interest rates.

Pros and Cons

Pros	Cons
Lower volatility than stocks	Lower potential returns than stocks
Reliable income from interest payments	Impacted heavily by interest rate changes
Good diversification tool	Less liquid compared to stocks and ETFs

How to Invest

- **Select a brokerage with bond offerings:** Look for platforms that provide easy access to bond markets.
- **Research yield curves and interest rates:** Study current interest rate trends to anticipate how they might impact bond prices.

- **Choose bonds with short maturities for trading:** Shorter-duration bonds are less sensitive to interest rate fluctuations, making them suitable for short-term traders.

Commodities

Commodities are physical assets—think gold, oil, and agricultural goods. Commodity prices are driven by global supply and demand dynamics, making them suitable for day traders who keep an eye on economic and geopolitical events (*Commodities Trading*, n.d.).

Features

- **Global demand influence:** Prices fluctuate based on supply chain events, geopolitical news, and even weather.
- **Hedge against inflation:** Commodity prices often rise during inflationary times, providing a shield against currency devaluation.
- **Leverage and high volatility:** Many commodity traders use leverage to maximize returns, but it also increases risk.

Common Strategies

- **Technical analysis:** Day traders use charts to predict short-term movements and capitalize on price volatility.

- **Supply and demand-based trading:** Events like droughts or oil production cuts can drastically change commodity prices, providing quick trading opportunities.

Pros and Cons

Pros	Cons
Inflation hedge	High leverage increases risk
High-profit potential	Commodity prices are highly unpredictable
Wide variety of options	Knowledge-intensive trading

How to Invest

- **Select a trading platform with commodity options:** Some brokers specialize in commodities, so choose a platform with low fees.
- **Stay updated on global news:** Commodity prices are highly reactive to current events, so stay informed on international developments.
- **Practice with futures and options:** Start with smaller trades using futures or options contracts to limit exposure.

Cryptocurrencies

Cryptocurrencies like Bitcoin or Ethereum are digital currencies. With 24/7 availability and high volatility, they're popular with day traders looking to take advantage of price swings. Crypto's unpredictable nature attracts traders who enjoy fast-paced, high-risk trades.

Features

- **High volatility:** Prices of cryptocurrencies can vary drastically within a single day, creating the potential for both profit and significant loss. This volatility can be rewarding for skilled traders who can quickly react to price swings but may be risky for those less experienced.
- **Blockchain technology:** Cryptocurrencies rely on blockchain technology, a decentralized, secure, and transparent ledger system that makes each

transaction traceable. This decentralized nature means cryptocurrencies aren't controlled by any single entity, adding to their appeal for traders looking for more autonomy.

- **Global accessibility:** Unlike traditional markets, cryptocurrency trading is available worldwide and around the clock. Traders can participate at any time, regardless of location, which adds flexibility and makes monitoring challenging for long periods.

Common Strategies

- **Scalping:** Scalpers in the crypto market try to capture small gains by trading frequently within minutes or seconds, capitalizing on tiny price movements.
- **Arbitrage:** Some traders use arbitrage, buying cryptocurrency on one exchange and selling it on another where the price is slightly higher. This requires fast decision-making and sophisticated software.
- **Range trading:** Using resistance and support levels, range traders look for opportunities when prices fluctuate between known high and low levels. This can be a solid choice in a relatively stable market phase.

Pros and Cons

Pros	Cons
High volatility can lead to fast gains	Extreme price swings can result in significant losses.
Decentralized and accessible 24/7	Unregulated, leading to potential scams or security risks
Many exchanges with relatively low transaction fees	Requires constant monitoring and understanding of digital technology

How to Invest

- **Choose a reliable exchange:** Start by choosing a reputable cryptocurrency exchange, like Coinbase, Binance, or Kraken, and set up an account with strong security measures, like two-factor authentication.
- **Fund your account:** Deposit funds, typically through a bank transfer or credit card, depending on the exchange's options.
- **Start with stable coins or major cryptos:** Beginners should start with well-known, less volatile options like Bitcoin or Ethereum before exploring more volatile altcoins.
- **Monitor and set alerts:** Given the market's constant activity, set price alerts and monitor news to stay aware of significant events that might affect cryptocurrency prices.
- **Consider a secure wallet:** For added security, store your cryptocurrency in a secure wallet, either a software wallet for short-term use or a hardware wallet for long-term holding (Deer, 2023).

Criteria for Selecting Trading Assets

Cryptocurrencies present a mix of excitement and risk, making them a high-reward option that requires sharp instincts and risk tolerance. This asset category can be highly rewarding for traders who enjoy a fast-paced market, but its volatility means it's also not for the faint-hearted.

Choosing the right asset to trade can be like choosing a restaurant for a first date. You want something reliable, ideally with good reviews, a solid reputation, and a menu that doesn't break the bank but promises quality. In the trading world, evaluating an asset before diving in is essential to ensure it aligns with your goals and risk tolerance. Below are some key criteria for assessing the quality of a trading asset.

Let's dive into the factors that traders should consider and take a look at what each criterion brings to the table (Robinson, 2018).

Quality Rating

A quality rating is the *Yelp review of* an asset. A high-quality rating indicates that an asset is like a highly rated restaurant: trusted, reliable, and usually meeting expectations. This score, often determined by rating agencies like Moody's or S&P, assesses a company or bond's creditworthiness or overall reliability.

- **Why it matters:** Quality ratings help traders gauge a company's financial health. Highly rated companies are usually more stable, while low-rated ones may be high-risk with potentially higher returns.

- **Tip:** If you want to balance risk and reward, look for assets with a minimum rating of BBB for bonds or equivalent ratings for other assets.

Financial Leverage

Financial leverage is like borrowing money to make a big splash, like a chef taking out a loan to open a second location. In finance, leverage is the amount of debt a company has taken on relative to its equity. Higher leverage can mean higher potential returns but also an increased risk, especially if the company struggles to manage its debt.

- **Why it matters:** A highly leveraged company might have an attractive growth potential but could struggle to make interest payments if earnings dip, which can affect its stock price.
- **Tip:** Check the debt-to-equity ratio. If it's high, ensure the company has stable cash flow to cover its debt. A ratio under 1.0 is often considered safe, though this varies by industry.

Company's Liquidity

Liquidity is like the flexibility of a restaurant menu: How easily can the company turn its assets into cash if needed? A liquid company can manage unexpected costs or downturns, which usually makes it a safer investment.

- **Why it matters:** Higher liquidity means a company can cover short-term liabilities without needing to take drastic steps, like selling off assets at a loss.

- **Tip:** Look for assets with a healthy current ratio (current assets/current liabilities) of at least 1.5. This ratio means the company can cover its debts comfortably, which is especially important in volatile markets.

Positive Earnings Growth

Positive earnings growth is like a popular restaurant chain that keeps opening new branches due to demand. Consistent growth in earnings indicates that the company is doing something right, either by increasing sales, expanding markets, or improving efficiency.

- **Why it matters**: A company with growing earnings is likely to see its stock price increase over time, which can lead to higher returns for traders.
- **Tip:** Review the earnings-per-share (EPS) growth rate over the past three to five years. Steady, upward-trending growth is a good indicator, while erratic growth might require further investigation.

Price-to-Earnings Ratio

The price-to-earnings (P/E) ratio is like checking a restaurant's menu prices before deciding if it's worth the visit. It shows how much you're paying for each dollar of earnings. A high P/E might mean the asset is *pricey or* that investors expect high future growth; a low P/E might signal undervaluation or potential issues.

- **Why it matters:** The P/E ratio helps traders understand whether a stock is overpriced, underpriced, or fairly valued based on its earnings.
- **Tip:** Compare the P/E ratio with the industry average to gauge if the asset is reasonably priced. A P/E ratio between 15 and 20 is typical for many industries, though tech stocks often have higher P/Es due to their growth potential.

Price-to-Book Ratio

The price-to-book (P/B) ratio compares the cost of a meal to the quality of its ingredients. It shows how much you pay relative to the company's net assets, giving insight into whether the stock is overvalued or undervalued.

- **Why it matters:** A lower P/B ratio, often under 1, may indicate undervaluation, particularly for well-established companies with significant assets. It's particularly useful for asset-heavy industries like real estate or manufacturing.
- **Tip:** If a stock has a low P/B ratio but high earnings and low debt, it may be a hidden gem. However, if both P/B and P/E are low, it could also mean the company is facing significant challenges.

Dividends

Dividends are like some restaurants' complimentary appetizers—a little extra value for your investment. Companies with strong cash flow often reward shareholders with dividends, providing a steady return even when stock prices fluctuate.

- **Why it matters:** Dividends offer an additional income stream, which can be especially valuable during volatile market periods when stock prices might be unstable.
- **Tip:** Look at the dividend yield (annual dividend per share/price per share) to understand the return on investment from dividends. A 2–4% yield is generally healthy; higher yields may signal higher risk if they exceed industry norms.

Practical Steps for Selecting Trading Assets Based on These Criteria

1. **Identify your goals and risk tolerance:** Determine if you want stable returns, high-growth potential, or dividend income. This will guide your criteria to prioritize.
2. **Research and screen assets:** Use online screening tools to filter assets based on quality rating, P/E ratio, P/B ratio, and other factors. Tools like Finviz and Morningstar and broker-provided filters help.
3. **Perform a fundamental analysis:** Look beyond ratios. Read financial statements, analyze recent performances, and check for industry-specific concerns or opportunities.
4. **Stay informed on economic trends:** Certain criteria, like leverage and liquidity, are more sensitive to economic shifts. For instance, high leverage might be a red flag if interest rates are rising.

5. **Diversify your portfolio:** Even with solid selection criteria, spreading investments across different sectors or asset types is wise to minimize risk.

When you understand and use these criteria, you can approach the selection of assets with a sharper focus and a clearer picture of each choice's strengths and potential pitfalls.

Whether you're drawn to the stability of low P/E stocks or the growth potential of high-quality ratings, each factor adds depth to your investment decision, helping you build a portfolio that aligns with your goals and appetite for risk (Robinson, 2018).

The next step is mastering the tools that can elevate your game. We'll look at the essential tools and platforms, including how to choose the right broker to support your trading journey.

Make a Difference with Your Review

UNLOCK THE POWER OF SHARING

"A candle loses nothing by lighting another candle."

James Keller

The world of day trading can be exciting, but it can also feel overwhelming when you're just starting. That's where *Day Trading Mastery Made Quick and Easy* comes in—to make the journey simpler and more enjoyable for everyone who dreams of mastering the markets.

Would you help someone like you—someone curious about day trading but unsure where to start?

My mission is to make day trading approachable, fun, and rewarding for all. But to reach more aspiring traders, I need your help and its much easier then you think to do so.

Most people pick their next read based on reviews. By leaving yours, you could help another reader decide to take the leap into day trading. Your words might be the encouragement someone needs that final push or words of encoragement:

- Take the first step in learning to trade.
- Build skills that could support their family.
- Start chasing financial freedom.
- Make their dream of trading come true.

It's easy to make a difference. It takes less than a minute, costs nothing, and could change someone's trading journey forever.

Just scan the QR code below:

If helping others succeed brings you joy, you're my kind of person. Thank you for supporting not just this book but the readers who will come after you.

With gratitude,

Daniel Fernell

SIX

Tools of the Trade

The best investment is in the tools of one's own trade.

Benjamin Franklin

Why Use Day Trading Tools?

Have you ever tried baking a cake without a recipe or fixing your car with a hammer? Sounds messy. The same goes for trading without the proper tools. You *can do* it, but you'd make it unnecessarily complicated. Trading tools are like kitchen gadgets or a toolbox —they simplify the process, help you avoid mistakes, and make you more efficient. Let's break it down.

Performing Calculations

Imagine cooking a big family dinner and needing to adjust the ingredient quantities for everyone. Would you trust yourself to eyeball it or reach for a measuring cup? In the trading world, tools like calculators and automated programs are those measuring cups, ensuring your calculations are precise. Whether it's figuring out potential profits or losses, these tools save you from doing complex math on your own.

Facilitating Stock Trades

Think of trading tools as your own "click-and-collect" system for the stock market. You can browse stocks, decide what you want, and hit the button—boom, transaction complete. Without these tools, you'd call brokers, check prices, and manually fill out forms. Trading platforms streamline this entire process so you can spend less time fumbling and more time making decisions.

Determining Which Stocks to Trade

Have you ever tried choosing a movie to watch when there are thousands of options? It could take hours! Trading tools help narrow your choices by providing filters and analytics pointing you toward stocks that match your interests and risk tolerance. They give you the "what's trending now" list for stocks, making decision-making smoother and faster.

Storing and Saving Certain Financial Assets

Think of trading tools like a high-tech filing cabinet. You wouldn't leave your important documents lying around the house, would you? These tools store your financial assets securely, ensuring everything stays in one place and is easily accessible. Moreover, some tools even offer cloud storage so you can access your portfolio from anywhere, anytime.

Researching Market and Economic Trends

Keeping up with the markets is like trying to stay on top of the latest fashion trends—they are constantly changing, and there's a lot to keep track of. Trading tools do the hard work for you by monitoring and analyzing market trends continuously so you don't have to read every economic report yourself. They give you the lowdown on what's happening and what it means for your trades.

Moving Funds

Transferring money between accounts, platforms, or even countries isn't easy, but trading tools make it as simple as transferring money between your savings and checking accounts. Like online banking for traders, these tools help move your funds swiftly, ensuring you can seize opportunities as soon as they arise (*Guide to 6-Day Trading Tools*, 2024).

Trading Platforms

Navigating this realm is like trying to steer a ship through stormy seas—there are many moving parts, and it's easy to get lost. That's where trading platforms come in, acting as your navigation system to help you chart the course. Several options are available, so you must know which platform to choose. Let's break down some of the best trading platforms and what makes them useful so you can find the right one for you.

Think of a trading platform like a smartphone—it needs to have the right apps, smooth functionality, and a user-friendly interface. The best trading platforms come loaded with features that make trading smoother, quicker, and more effective. Here's what to keep an eye on (Folger, 2023):

Real-time market data: Like live updates during a football match, this feature ensures you're always in the know.

Low fees: No one likes hidden charges, and with many platforms offering lower trading fees, you can keep more of your hard-earned money.

User-friendly interface: Whether you're a pro or a beginner, the platform should feel intuitive and easy to navigate.

Customer support: Imagine having a coach you can call any time for tips! That's what excellent customer support feels like.

Benefits of Trading Through a Brokerage Firm

Using a brokerage firm is like having a personal assistant to handle the tough stuff while you focus on the bigger picture. It offers several key advantages:

- **Liquidity:** Have you ever tried selling something online only to wait forever for a buyer? Trading with a brokerage firm ensures you don't worry about finding buyers or sellers. With high liquidity, your trades happen quickly so you're not left waiting when you're ready to act.
- **Access to markets:** Think of a brokerage as your VIP pass to all the cool places. They give you access to a wide range of markets—stocks, forex, commodities, and more—so you have plenty of opportunities to diversify your investments.
- **Lower fees:** You wouldn't overpay for a cup of coffee, so why overpay to trade? Many online brokerages offer lower fees than traditional brokers, making it more affordable to get in the game without eroding your profits.
- **Transparency:** Nobody likes surprises, especially when it comes to money. Brokerage firms offer transparency with clear transaction histories, account reports, and real-time tracking so you know exactly where you stand at all times.
- **Customer support:** Need help or have a question at 2 a.m.? Many brokerage platforms offer 24/7 customer support, which is like having a personal advisor available whenever you need guidance.

- **High leverage:** Leverage in trading is a bit like getting a loan to buy a house. You can trade more than what's in your account, potentially boosting your profits. But, like loans, leverage should be handled carefully, as it can magnify both gains and losses.
- **Monitor investments all the time:** Thanks to mobile apps, you can monitor your investments even while sipping a latte at your favorite café. Day trading platforms give you constant access to your portfolio so you never miss a beat.
- **Regulation:** Using a regulated brokerage firm is like choosing a certified, well-reviewed contractor for an extensive home renovation—you know they're legit and held to strict standards. Regulated brokers ensure your funds are safe and follow industry rules.

Top Brokerage Firms

Picking a firm is like choosing your ride—you want something reliable, easy to handle, and packed with features that suit your needs. Luckily, plenty of options are available, each with its own perks and quirks. Let's look at some of the best brokerage firms around so you can find the one that feels just right for you!

*E*TRADE*

E*TRADE is like the Swiss Army knife of brokerage firms with a little bit of everything for everyone: It's great for beginners but packed with enough tools to satisfy seasoned traders. From stocks and options to mutual funds and futures, you can do it all here, and its user-friendly mobile app allows you to trade on the go.

Interactive Brokers IBKR Pro

If you love all the bells and whistles, IBKR Pro is for you. This platform is for serious traders who want access to global markets and professional-grade tools. It's like driving a high-performance sports car—it's powerful, but you'll need to know how to handle it to get the most out of it.

Fidelity

For the cautious and steady trader, Fidelity is like a luxury SUV—comfortable, safe, and full of features you didn't even know you needed. Its robust research tools and customer service make it perfect for long-term investors. Plus, there are zero commissions on many trades!

Charles Schwab

Charles Schwab is the family car of brokers. Whether you're a new driver or a seasoned pro, this platform has something for everyone. Schwab offers an excellent balance of low fees, a wide range of investment options, and helpful customer support to guide your journey.

Webull

Webull is like the sleek, stylish electric car of the brokerage world—modern, efficient, and ideal for tech-savvy traders. With zero commissions and an intuitive app, it's an excellent choice for anyone looking to trade stocks, ETFs, and crypto without breaking the bank.

SoFi Active Investing

For those who want to dip their toes into investing while managing student loans or saving for a house, SoFi is like a budget—friendly hybrid vehicle designed for multitasking. Its commission-free trading platform is easy to use, and its app gives you access to other financial services all in one place.

TradeStation

If you're into technical analysis, TradeStation should be your go-to platform. It's like the dashboard of a race car. It's built for speed and precision, offering advanced tools and real-time data that help traders analyze trends and patterns. It's a solid option for those who like to dive deep into data.

Zacks Trade

For any research junkies out there, Zacks Trade is your research assistant, helping you make informed decisions with a wealth of resources and data. It's perfect for investors who want to get into the nitty-gritty of stock analysis before hitting the "buy" button.

Firstrade

Firstrade is the trusty old sedan—simple, affordable, and reliable. It doesn't have all the flash of some of the others, but it gets the job done for zero-commission trading and a straightforward experience.

Ally Invest

Ally Invest is like that dependable friend who always comes through when you need them. It offers a seamless experience for investors with checking, savings, and trading accounts all in one place. This is the one if you want a platform that integrates well with your everyday banking.

Merrill Edge® Self-Directed

For those who like the comfort of banking with a household name, Merrill Edge® Self-Directed is like upgrading to first class with your frequent flyer miles. It's tied to Bank of America, so if you're already a customer, you'll enjoy perks like seamless account integration and great research tools (Broking, 2023).

Choosing a Broker

Choosing a broker is a lot like picking out shoes: Sure, they all do the job, but you want something that fits your style, is comfortable, and works for your needs. Here's a quick guide on what to consider before making your decision:

- **Fees:** Just like you'd compare price tags, you'd need to check out the fee structures of different firms. Look for platforms with low commissions or no fees on specific trades—it'll save you money in the long run.
- **Trading tools:** If you love fancy gadgets, ensure your platform has all the technical tools you need. Whether it's real-time data, advanced charting, or research resources, pick one that offers the features that suit your trading style.
- **Customer support:** Have you ever had a question and couldn't get an answer right away? It's frustrating! That's why customer support is essential. Whether via live chat, email, or a phone call, ensure the brokerage offers solid support in case you run into issues.
- **Investment options:** If you like variety, choose a broker that gives you access to a wide range of investments—stocks, ETFs, mutual funds, options, or even crypto. The more options, the more diversified your portfolio can be.
- **Platform usability:** No one wants to spend hours figuring out how to place a trade. Look for platforms that are easy to navigate, whether you're on a computer or mobile app. A clean, intuitive interface makes trading more enjoyable and less stressful.
- **Research resources:** If you like to do your homework before making a decision, look for platforms that offer robust research tools—analyst ratings, reports, and data—that can help you make smarter trading choices.

- **Regulation and security:** Ensure your chosen broker is regulated correctly and follows industry standards. You wouldn't trust your money with just anyone, would you? A regulated broker ensures your funds are safe and secure.
- **Leverage and margin:** If you want to take your trades to the next level, check if the broker offers leverage or margin trading. But be cautious: While it can amplify gains, it can also increase losses. It is like turbo-boosting your car—exciting, but you must handle it carefully!

Market Analysis Tools

If you've ever tried navigating through a crowded flea market, you know how helpful it is to get real-time information, like which stalls have the best deals and which are running out of your favorite snacks. The trading market is your flea market; real-time market data is your inside scoop. This info lets you make quick, informed decisions differentiating between a great trade and a missed opportunity. Let's dive into market analysis tools, starting with real-time market data.

What Is It?

Real-time market data is like checking the weather report before heading out—you get the most current information available. In trading, this data tells you exactly what's happening in the market at that very moment, from the latest stock prices to trading volumes. Think of it as your live feed of the stock market, letting you see every little fluctuation in prices as they happen.

You'd trade with one eye without real-time data, relying on outdated info. That's like showing up at a party after all the good snacks are gone. Using real-time market data keeps you in the loop and lets you make informed decisions faster.

Real-Time vs. 15-Minute Delayed Stock Quotes: What's the Difference?

Imagine driving on a highway with two different navigation systems: One gives you turn-by-turn directions in real-time, while the other shows you where traffic was 15 minutes ago. Which one would you trust more to avoid traffic jams?

That's the difference between the two. Real-time quotes tell you the exact price of a stock the moment you check it, whereas delayed quotes show you what the price was 15 minutes ago, like using old news to decide on a fast-moving market. Real-time quotes are essential for day traders who need to act quickly, while delayed quotes are more useful for those taking a more leisurely approach to investing.

What's Included in a Typical Real-Time Quote?

A real-time quote is packed with crucial information that helps you make sense of the market. Here's what you can expect to see:

- **Stock symbol:** This is the company's unique identifier (like its nickname) in the market, such as AAPL for Apple or TSLA for Tesla.
- **Latest stock price:** This tells you the most recent price the stock was traded at—your GPS for determining market movement.
- **Trading volume:** This number shows how many shares of the stock have been traded so far. Think of it like the foot traffic at a busy market stall—high volume means a lot of action!
- **52-week highs and lows:** These are the highest and lowest prices the stock has reached in the past year. It's like checking a temperature record—you'll know if the stock is at a high point or a low point.
- **Bid and ask price:** The bid price is what buyers are willing to pay for the stock, while the ask price is what sellers are asking for. The difference between them, known as the "spread," can tell you how easy or challenging it'll be to buy or sell that stock.
- **Underlying stock exchange:** This shows where the stock is being traded, like the New York Stock Exchange (aka NYSE) or the National Association of Security Dealers Automated Quotations (aka Nasdaq) Stock Market.

Benefits of Real-Time Data Analytics

- **Provides access to valuable market data without delay:** Real-time data lets you act quickly on stock movements, which is crucial for day traders looking to capitalize on small price changes.
- **Addresses operational problems promptly:** If something's not working right, whether it's the stock market or your trading software, real-time data can flag the issue immediately so you can fix it.
- **Monitors your trading infrastructure:** Think of it as your trading dashboard—it tracks everything in real-time, so if there's a hiccup, you know immediately.
- **Facilitates better, faster decisions:** When the clock's ticking, you need information you can trust. Real-time data helps you make decisions on the fly with confidence.
- **Spotting trends and potential issues early can cut down on costs, allowing you to** avoid costly mistakes and streamline your trades.
- **Helps prepare forecasts:** Like a weather forecast for the stock market, real-time data helps you predict future movements based on current trends.
- **Keeps track of everything**: From employees in a company to departments, real-time data ensures you have the complete picture at all times.
- **Improves customer service:** Quick access to real-time data can help enhance the overall customer experience for brokers and financial service providers by addressing issues faster.

How to Use It

Here's a quick guide to get you started:

1. **Watch for stock movements:** Keep an eye on how stocks move throughout the day. If a stock you're interested in starts climbing rapidly, you can jump in before it gets too high.
2. **Analyze trading volume:** High volume can indicate strong interest in a stock, which often means higher price volatility—perfect for day trading!
3. **Follow the bid-ask spread:** A smaller spread means the stock is easier to trade. If you see a wider spread, you might want to hold off until things settle down.
4. **Use alerts:** Many trading platforms allow you to set real-time alerts for specific stock prices. This way, you don't have to monitor the market 24/7. Your platform will let you know when it's time to act.
5. **Leverage analytics:** Use real-time data analytics to study market trends and make educated predictions. Like a chess game, the more you anticipate your next move, the better your chances of success.

Technical Analysis Tools

Imagine you're trying to figure out the best time to jump into the ocean for a swim. You don't want to dive in when the waves are too high or the water's too cold. In the trading world, technical analysis tools are like your ocean forecast—they help you decide when the conditions are just right for making your move in the market. Let's break down the basics and how they can help you navigate the waves of trading (Hayes, 2021).

What Does Technical Trade Analysis Involve?

At its core, technical trade analysis is like studying the rhythm of the market. It involves analyzing historical price data, charts, and market trends to predict where prices might go in the future. Instead of focusing on a company's financial health or the state of the economy, technical analysis zeroes in on price movements and patterns.

It's like trying to guess the next step in a dance routine. By observing previous moves, you can make an educated guess about what comes next. Traders use these patterns to determine the best time to buy or sell a stock.

Benefits of Technical Analysis

It comes with some pretty nifty perks:

- **Timing is everything:** Just like jumping into the ocean at the right moment, technical analysis helps you time your trades better. It's all about knowing when to dive in and when to stay out.
- **No need for company gossip:** Unlike fundamental analysis, you don't need to keep up with a company's earnings reports or news. Instead, you're looking purely at market trends and data, which is often quicker and less complex.

- **Flexible and versatile:** You can apply technical analysis across various markets—stocks, forex, commodities, you name it! The principles are the same, no matter what you're trading.

Limitations of Technical Market Analysis

Technical analysis isn't a crystal ball. It has its limitations, just like any trading strategy:

- **Not foolproof:** Simply because a pattern worked in the past doesn't guarantee it'll work in the future. Markets can be unpredictable, so you must always be prepared for surprises.
- **Needs time and practice:** Like learning to read the ocean's tides, mastering technical analysis takes practice. You'll need time to understand how to read charts and use the tools properly.
- **Can't predict big news events:** If a company suddenly announces a breakthrough or disaster, technical analysis won't see it coming. It focuses purely on price movements, not the external factors driving them.

Key Concepts

Let's cover a few key concepts that form the foundation of technical analysis:

- **Trends:** Markets often move in patterns called trends—upward, downward, or sideways. Identifying these trends is crucial for knowing when to buy or sell.

- **Support and resistance:** These are like invisible barriers in the market. Support is the price level where a stock tends to stop falling, while resistance is the level where it stops rising.
- **Volume:** This measures how much of a stock is being traded. High volume can signal a strong market move, while low volume means fewer people are buying or selling.

Popular Technical Analysis Tools

Let's examine some of the most popular tools traders use to understand market trends and make better decisions. Each tool helps answer one question: "Is this the right time to jump in?"

1. **Relative Strength Index**: Think of it as a stock's fitness tracker—it tells you if a stock is overbought (too expensive) or oversold (a bargain). If the relative strength index (RSI) value is over 70, the stock might be overbought, meaning a price dip could be coming. Below 30? It might be oversold and due for a rise.
2. **Moving Average Convergence Divergence:** This is like your market trend compass. It helps traders spot changes in momentum and predict when a stock might change direction. Think of moving average convergence divergence (MACD) as a radar that shows if the market's momentum is speeding up or slowing down.

3. **Stochastic Oscillator:** Imagine you're at a party, and the room gets super crowded. That's an overbought market. If it starts to empty out, that's an oversold market). The stochastic oscillator helps you gauge this crowd density. It compares a stock's closing price to its price range over a specific period, signaling if a stock is being over- or under-traded.
4. **Average Directional Index:** This index measures the strength of a trend. It's like checking how strong the wind is before deciding whether to fly your kite. If it is above 25, the trend is strong. Below 20? The trend is weak or nonexistent.
5. **Fibonacci Retracement:** Fibonacci is a fancy way of finding potential reversal points in the market. It's based on a mathematical sequence traders use to predict areas of support or resistance. Think of it as your market GPS that helps you move toward key turning points.
6. **Moving Average:** A moving average smooths out price data, creating a clearer view of the overall trend. It's like using a filter to make a fuzzy picture clearer. This average helps you determine if the price increases or decreases over time.
7. **On-Balance Volume:** This tool looks at volume to determine price momentum. If more people are buying a stock, the volume rises; if more are selling, it drops. Think of it as watching the tide go in and out. A rising on-balance volume suggests that a stock price might follow suit.
8. **TradingView:** This popular online charting platform lets you use multiple technical analysis tools in one place. It's like your all-in-one Swiss Army knife for

trading, with charts, indicators, and community insights all in one dashboard.

9. **Aroon Indicator:** Aroon helps you spot the start of a new trend or the end of an old one. It's like a trend alarm clock, waking you up when it's time to act. It measures how long it has been since a stock reached its highest or lowest point within a certain period (Hayes, 2021).

Technical analysis doesn't guarantee success, but it gives you the tools to read market conditions like a seasoned sailor navigating rough seas. By learning how to use these tools effectively, you can make smarter, more informed decisions and feel more confident as you dive into the trading world (Carey, 2024).

Fundamental Analysis Tools

Think of fundamental analysis as a detective trying to crack a case. Instead of focusing on stock price patterns or market trends, you're diving deep into the company's health, management, and overall market performance. This approach helps you understand whether a stock is truly valuable, like Sherlock Holmes piecing together clues to solve a mystery. Let's break down the basics for day traders and how to use them to uncover the story behind each stock (*Fundamental Analysis Tools: Top Tools for Investors,* n.d.).

What Does Fundamental Analysis Entail?

In short, it's all about looking at the bigger picture. You're not just interested in stock charts or price fluctuations. Instead, you're examining the core elements that make a company tick.

You wouldn't buy a house based solely on its fresh paint job (the stock price), right? You'd want to check the foundation, the plumbing, and the neighborhood's safety. Fundamental analysis is similar to home inspection—it digs deep into a company's structure to assess its true worth.

Essential Tools

Each offers critical clues, helping you decide whether a stock is worth buying.

1. **Financial reports:** Financial reports are like report cards. They include balance sheets, income statements, and cash flow statements, giving you a clear idea of performance. If a company consistently pulls A's, it's likely a solid investment.
2. **Effectiveness of management:** A company with poor leadership is like a ship with a lousy captain—it's bound to go off course. Look for information about how well the company is being steered, how experienced the leadership team is, and what the leadership and company's track record is.
3. **Asset management:** Is the company making the most out of its assets or are resources wasted? Just like you'd want to know if a restaurant is managing its ingredients well, you'd want to know if the company is putting its assets to good use.
4. **Demand:** How much is the demand for the company's products or services? High demand is an excellent indicator that the business is likely to grow. Imagine investing in a bakery: If their donuts are flying off the shelves, that's a good sign.
5. **Company's press releases:** These are the official statements companies put out about new products, strategies, or financial results. Reading them is like getting updates directly from the horse's mouth.
6. **Global industry review:** Is the industry growing or shrinking? For example, companies like Apple and Samsung thrived during the smartphone boom. But investing in an industry that's losing steam is like betting on a horse that is already slowing down.

7. **Trade agreements and external policies:** Government policies or trade agreements can significantly impact a company's growth. Think of them as the weather conditions before a race: You'd want to know whether the forecast is in your favor.
8. **News releases:** Staying on top of the latest news gives you real-time updates on things that could affect a company like product recalls, lawsuits, or scandals. It's like hearing about a plot twist just before the final chapter—it's always good to know.
9. **Competitor analysis:** Just like in sports, knowing how the competition is doing can give you insights into your team. If competitors are outperforming, it might be time to re-evaluate.

Widely Used Fundamental Analysis Tools

Here are some of the most commonly used tools that can give you a clear picture of a company's financial health and prospects:

1. **EPS:** Think of it as the company's productivity score —how much profit they generate for each share of stock. A higher EPS generally signals better performance.
2. **P/E Ratio:** This ratio tells you how expensive a stock is compared to its earnings. It's like comparing the price of two cars: One might be more expensive, but does it offer better value for what you're paying?

3. **Return on Equity:** This is the company's ability to generate profit using shareholders' money. If you were an investor, you'd want to know how well your money is being put to work.
4. **P/B Ratio:** This compares the company's market value to its book value (what it's worth on paper). A lower P/B ratio could mean the stock is undervalued —a potential bargain!
5. **Beta:** Beta measures how volatile a stock is compared to the market. If you don't like roller coasters, you might want a stock with a low beta—it's like a calm ride compared to a wild one.
6. **Price-to-Sales Ratio:** This ratio compares a company's stock price to its revenue. It's an excellent way to see how much you pay for each sales dollar.
7. **Dividend Payout Ratio:** This measures how much of a company's earnings are paid out as dividends. High payout ratios could indicate strong performance, but they might also suggest the company isn't reinvesting enough for future growth.
8. **Dividend Yield Ratio:** The yield shows how much cash you're getting back from your investment in the form of dividends. High dividend yield stocks may be attractive if you like a steady income stream.
9. **Projected Earnings Growth:** This forecast shows how much the company's earnings are expected to grow. It's like seeing the weather forecast—sunny skies ahead usually mean better opportunities!

Automation Tools

Algorithmic trading, or *algo trading,* is like setting your coffee machine to brew at 6 a.m.—you set the rules, and it executes trades automatically. It involves using computer programs to follow pre-set criteria, like when to buy or sell stocks, based on price, timing, or market volume. Let's break it down:

What Is It?

Algorithmic trading involves trading done by computers, not humans. You create rules, and the algorithm follows them to make trades for you. It's fast, efficient, and can execute trades in milliseconds—much faster than any human could (*Introduction to Trade Execution Algorithms,* 2019)

How Does It Work?

It works by using historical data and complex algorithms to make trading decisions. Once certain conditions are met (for example, if a stock price hits a certain level), the program executes the trade without hesitation, like your coffee machine kicking into action at a specific time.

Pros and Cons

Pros

- **Speed:** Algorithms can execute trades in milliseconds, taking advantage of the slightest movements.

- **Emotionless:** Computers don't get scared or greedy —they follow the rules without emotion.
- **Backtesting:** You can test your algorithm on historical data to see if it would have worked in the past.

Cons

- **Complexity:** Setting up an algorithm requires some serious technical know-how.
- **Over-Optimization:** Sometimes, algorithms need to be more finely tuned to past data, which may not reflect future market conditions.

Common Trade Execution Algorithms

- **Time-weighted average Price: This algorithm aims** to execute trades evenly over a specific period, avoiding large price changes.
- **Volume-weighted average Price:** This strategy seeks to execute trades in proportion to the trading volume at different times of the day.
- **Percent of Value:** This algorithm adjusts its trading volume based on the stock's price movements throughout the day (Kokaz, 2020).

Trading Bots

Imagine having a tireless assistant who never sleeps, always keeps an eye on the market, and trades for you when you're too busy or even when you're fast asleep. That's what a trading bot is—a supercharged robot assistant to help with your trades. But like any good assistant, it comes with its perks and quirks. Let's look at how they work, their benefits, risks, and some tips for getting the most out of them (Putzhammer, 2022).

What Are They?

Trading bots are like chefs who follow your recipe to the letter. You set the ingredients (your strategy), and the bot does the cooking (executing trades) based on those instructions. A trading bot is an automated software program that buys and sells assets on your behalf based on a set of predefined rules.

You can customize these rules to be as simple or complex as you like, ranging from "buy when the price drops by X%" to "execute trades only when the price, volume, and news sentiment align."

Benefits

- **Speed:** Bots can execute trades in milliseconds. Humans can't compete with the lightning-fast decisions bots can make.
- **Accuracy:** A bot doesn't have *off* days and never misreads the numbers. It follows your rules exactly, every time, without emotion or fatigue.
- **24/7 Operation:** The markets don't sleep and neither does your bot. Whether it's 2 a.m. or a holiday, your bot can keep monitoring and trading even when you're on vacation.

- **Risk management:** Bots can adhere to predefined risk parameters much better than humans. If you tell a bot to sell if a stock drops by 5%, the bot won't hesitate to second-guess that decision.
- **Backtesting and optimization:** Bots allow you to backtest strategies using historical data to see how they performed. It's like having a crystal ball that shows you what could've happened in the past.

Types of Trading Bots

Just as there are different types of chefs, there are also different kinds of trading bots, each designed for a specific task.

1. **Trend-following bots:** These bots ride the wave of a trend. If the market is going up, they'll keep buying; if it's going down, they'll keep selling.
2. **News-based bots:** These bots read the headlines and make trades based on market-moving news. It's like having a bot that listens to gossip and reacts before anyone else.
3. **Arbitrage bots:** Arbitrage bots are the bargain hunters of the trading world. They look for price differences in different markets and exploit those discrepancies. Imagine buying sneakers at a discount in one store and selling them for a profit in another. Arbitrage bots do the same but with assets.
4. **Mean-reversion bots:** These bots believe prices will eventually return to their average like a rubber band snapping back into place. When prices deviate too

much from the norm, they trade accordingly, expecting things to return to balance.

5. **High-frequency bots:** These bots are the flashiest of them all. They execute a high volume of trades at ultra-fast speeds, taking advantage of tiny price changes within seconds. They are like day traders on steroids.

Risks Associated With Trading Bots

Trading bots have their perks, but they're not perfect. Before handing over the keys to your trading kingdom, you should learn about the risks.

Over-optimization: A bot that's too finely tuned to past data might not perform well in the real market. This is like making the perfect cake in a test kitchen but ending up with a burnt one when you try it at home.

Technical failures: Bots rely on technology, but tech isn't always perfect. Power outages, server crashes, or internet issues can cause your bot to malfunction, potentially costing you money.

Market risks: Bots can't predict black swan events—unforeseen market crashes or extreme volatility. In such situations, they may continue to trade according to their rules, even when human intuition says, "Hold off!"

Lack of flexibility: Bots don't adapt well to sudden market changes unless reprogrammed. They're like a chef who keeps adding salt even when you've asked for none—once programmed, they follow the instructions to the letter, for better or worse.

Operational risks: If the bot is poorly designed or its algorithm has flaws, it could make costly errors. You wouldn't want a chef who confuses sugar with salt, right?

Tips for Building a Trading Bot

If you're adventurous and want to create your own bot, here are a few tips:

- **Keep it simple:** Start with basic recipes before you try complex gourmet meals. Begin with a simple trading strategy and build from there.
- **Use reliable data**: Make sure your bot has access to high-quality, real-time data. Feeding it insufficient data is like giving a chef spoiled ingredients: You can't expect a good outcome.
- **Test, test, and test again:** Backtest your bot's strategy on historical data and run it in a simulated environment before unleashing it in the live market. It's like practicing a recipe before serving it at a dinner party.

Keeping an Eye on Your Bot

Once your bot is up and running, don't just let it run wild. Here are a few tips to monitor and manage it effectively:

- **Monitor regularly:** Check your bot's performance to ensure it's working as expected. Even the best assistants need supervision from time to time.

- **Set fail-safes:** Use stop-loss orders or set limits to prevent it from going rogue. It's like having a smoke detector in your kitchen—better safe than sorry.
- **Keep it updated:** Markets change and so should your bot's strategy. Regularly tweak and update the algorithm to keep it relevant, just like you'd update a recipe to suit changing tastes.

Community Traders

You can get into a kitchen and cook a meal solo, but wouldn't it be great to have others around you to share tips, ideas, and perhaps a few trade secrets? Well, *trading communities are* like your cooking class, filled with fellow traders sharing insights, strategies, and encouragement to make your journey smoother. Let's dive into the world of trading communities and discover how joining one can spice up your day trading.

What Is a Trading Community?

It's like a group chat for traders—a space, online or in person, where traders of all levels come together to exchange ideas, strategies, and experiences. It's a supportive environment where you can ask questions, learn from others, and even share your own trading victories and mishaps (*What Is a Trader's Community?*, 2023).

Types of Trading Communities

Just as there are different cooking styles, there are different types of trading communities catering to various needs.

1. **Social media groups:** Think Facebook groups, Reddit threads, or Twitter discussions. These groups are more casual, like grabbing fast food with friends and chatting about the market (Nelson, 2023).
2. **Paid membership communities:** Like a specialized cooking class, these communities offer premium resources, expert insights, and advanced tools. It's an investment that's often worth it for serious traders.
3. **Mentorship programs:** Imagine having a private cooking coach. Mentorship communities offer one-on-one guidance or group mentorship from experienced traders. They are perfect for those looking for personalized advice.

Why Should You Join a Trading Community?

Why cook alone when you can have a whole team helping you? Joining a trading community can fast-track your success in many ways:

- **Learn from others:** Trading is tricky, but with a community, you don't have to reinvent the wheel. You can learn from the mistakes and successes of others.

- **Access exclusive resources:** Communities offer exclusive content, such as trading signals, webinars, and live trading sessions, that you won't find elsewhere.
- **Receive emotional support:** Trading can be an emotional roller coaster. In a community, you'll find people who've been through the same ups and downs and can offer much-needed encouragement.
- **Find networking opportunities:** Whether you're a newbie or a pro, meeting other traders opens up collaboration opportunities, partnerships, or simply finding a good mentor.

Finding the Right Community

Not all trading communities are created equal, so here are a few things to keep in mind when picking yours:

1. **Check the community's focus:** Are you into day trading, swing trading, or long-term investing? Find a community that matches your style and goals.
2. **Look for engagement:** A dead community won't help. Ensure the group is active with regular discussions, live sessions, and responsive members.
3. **Examine the expertise level:** Some communities cater to beginners, while others are filled with seasoned traders. Choose a space where you can learn at your own pace.
4. **Consider the costs:** Free communities are great, but paid ones might offer more structured resources. Decide what fits your budget and needs.

Once you've found your ideal trading community, joining is as easy as following a recipe:

1. **Sign up:** Whether joining a social media group or registering on a dedicated platform, most communities require a simple sign-up.
2. **Meet the requirements:** Some communities may have specific criteria like a minimum trading experience level or membership fees.
3. **Introduce yourself:** Like bringing a dish to a potluck, introduce yourself and share a bit about your trading background. It's a great way to start conversations and get to know others.

Hot Keys

Think of hotkeys as your shortcut to speeding up tasks. Like the kitchen gadgets that make chopping, mixing, and measuring faster, hotkeys help you buy, sell, and navigate the market with just a few keystrokes.

What Are They?

Hotkeys are pre-programmed keyboard shortcuts that allow you to execute trades faster. Instead of manually clicking through menus, you can press a combination of keys to place an order or adjust your position in the blink of an eye.

Benefits

- **Speed:** When the market's moving fast, every second counts. Hotkeys let you execute trades in an instant, saving you valuable time.
- **Precision:** Clicking around in a panic can lead to mistakes. Hotkeys ensure you're hitting exactly what you want, no more or less.
- **Customizability:** You can tailor hotkeys to fit your specific trading needs, just like customizing your favorite dish.

Types

- **Buy and sell:** These are your bread and butter, letting you quickly buy or sell assets with a single keystroke.
- **Stop-loss/take-profit orders:** Set your stop-loss or take-profit levels with ease to manage risk in real-time.
- **Cancel orders:** If you've ever wanted to "undo" a trade faster than you can say "whoops," this hotkey is for you.

Guide on Setting Hot Keys

- **Start with the basics:** Assign hotkeys to essential actions like buying, selling, and canceling orders.
- **Test before you trade:** Like practicing a new recipe before serving it to guests, test your hotkeys on a demo account to ensure they work as expected (Cameron, 2015).

Best Practices for Using Hotkeys

- **Keep it simple:** Don't go overboard. Stick to a few essential hotkeys to avoid confusion during busy trading periods.
- **Stay organized:** Just like keeping a tidy kitchen, label your hotkeys clearly so you always know what each one does (*Trading With Hot Keys Best Practices*, 2022).

Real-Time Watchlist Scanners

A real-time watchlist scanner is on your radar. It scans the market for stocks that match specific criteria, helping you zero in on opportunities in real-time.

What Is It?

It's like setting up an alert system that monitors the market, sifting through thousands of stocks and only highlighting those that meet your customized criteria. This scanner constantly updates, allowing you to catch profitable moves as they happen.

Why Use a Watchlist Scanner?

A watchlist scanner saves time and eliminates the guesswork. Without it, keeping an eye on potential opportunities would be like tracking dozens of quicksilver marbles rolling across the floor.

How to Create a Watchlist Scanner

First, outline your trading criteria by setting filters like price range, market sector, or volatility level. Many trading platforms allow you to set these filters, providing a tailored list that updates in real-time.

Using Your Watchlist Scanner

With your scanner live, watch how it catches stocks that fit your chosen criteria, helping you react quickly to market shifts. This tool is most powerful when regularly adjusted to fit current market conditions.

Chart Indicators

Reading charts is essential for making informed trading decisions. Trading charts are like snapshots of stock performance over time, showing patterns that can signal when to buy or sell.

Types of Trading Charts

- **Line chart:** The simplest chart, a line chart connects closing prices over a set period. It's a quick overview of a stock's general trend.

- **Bar chart:** Bar charts add more depth and show a stock's open, close, high, and low prices, giving you more details on daily price movement.

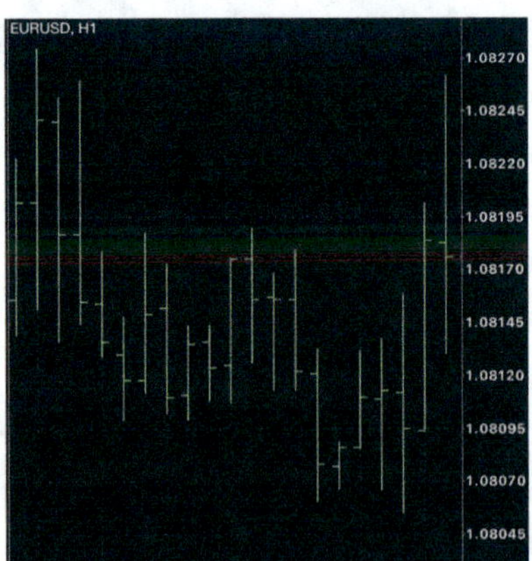

- **Candlestick chart**: A favorite of many traders, this chart uses colored "candlesticks" to show open, closed, high, and low values within specific timeframes. Its visual clarity makes it easier to interpret price momentum and trends at a glance.

Choosing a Day Trading Tool

Selecting the right trading tool can make or break your day trading strategy. Here's what to keep in mind:

- **Platform independence:** Ensure your tool can be used across multiple devices so you're not tethered to one setup.
- **Personal needs for day trading:** Whether focused on specific industries, low-volume stocks, or frequent trades, choose a tool that supports your style.

- **Analytical features:** Some tools offer advanced analysis with detailed charting, backtesting, and customizable alerts, which can improve your decision-making process.
- **Additional features**: Look for extras that support your workflow, such as order routing options, quick trade executions, and integration with other apps or data sources.

With the right tools, watchlist scanners, and chart indicators, you can develop a trading strategy that's as fast-paced and effective as the market itself.

SEVEN

Strategies That Make a Difference

However beautiful the strategy, you should occasionally look at the results.

Winston Churchill

Day Trading Strategies

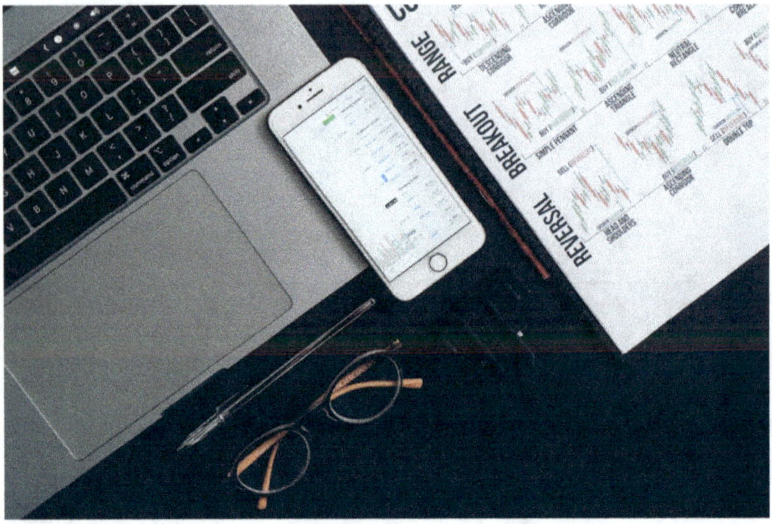

Some traders hop in and out of positions within the same day, aiming to catch price swings like surfers waiting for the perfect wave. Here are some popular day trading strategies, how they work, potential risks, and tips to make the most of each approach (Woods, 2016).

Reversal Trading Strategy

- **How it works:** Reversal trading focuses on spotting when a stock's price is about to change direction—like timing a U-turn. Traders look for signals that a downward trend is bottoming out (or an upward trend is topping out) to catch the wave as it reverses.
- **Risks:** False signals are common; if a "reversal" doesn't materialize, traders can get "stuck in the wrong direction."

- **Tips:** Use volume indicators to help confirm a true reversal. Strong volume often signals that a reversal has solid backing, increasing the odds that the price will change direction as expected (Cameron, 2022).

Engulfing Candlestick Pullback

- **How it works:** This strategy relies on "engulfing" candlesticks that cover or exceed the range of the previous candlestick, signaling strong market movement. It's like spotting a big fish in a pond—this pattern shows interest and momentum.
- **Risks:** Engulfing patterns can be unreliable on smaller time frames, making timing essential.
- **Tips:** Use larger time frames (like 15-minute or 1-hour charts) to increase reliability and combine with trend indicators to confirm market strength before entry (Capre, 2012).

Supply and Demand Zone Trading

- **How it works:** This approach seeks out "zones" where prices have historically stalled or reversed due to supply or demand imbalances. Think of it as shopping: You're buying low in the demand zone and selling high in the supply zone.
- **Risks:** Markets don't always respect historical supply and demand zones, especially during periods of high volatility.
- **Tips:** Look for strong price action within these zones to validate trades and avoid trading during

unpredictable events that can disrupt supply-demand behavior.

Daily Open and Session Momentum

- **How it works:** This strategy leverages the momentum of the opening session when the market first reacts to news or overnight events. Like the morning caffeine boost, the day's opening is often lively and sets the trend for the rest of the day.
- **Risks:** Early momentum can be misleading if it quickly fizzles out.
- **Tips:** Focus on high-volume stocks, which tend to react more strongly to morning momentum and use real-time news to gauge direction.

Daily High-Low Trend-Following Strategy

- **How it works:** A trend-following strategy involves spotting and following the daily highs or lows to ride ongoing trends. Imagine hopping on a moving train: Catching an existing movement rather than anticipating a shift.
- **Risks:** Trends can reverse suddenly, especially when driven by news.
- **Tips:** Use a trailing stop to lock in profits while giving the trend enough room to move, and be ready to exit if signs of reversal appear (Toyco, 2023).

Scalping Strategy

- **How it works:** Scalping is a fast-paced strategy in which traders make quick trades to earn small, frequent profits. It's like grabbing handfuls of popcorn—small bites but lots of them!
- **Risks:** Requires precision and a steady focus, as small movements can quickly lead to losses.
- **Tips:** Focus on highly liquid assets, use tight stop losses, and ensure your broker offers low transaction fees since you'll be making many trades.

Breakout Trading Strategy

- **How it works:** In breakout trading, you wait for a stock to break through a critical level, which signals the potential for a strong movement. It's like waiting for a horse to bolt out of the gate.
- **Risks:** False breakouts are common, leading to losses if the movement doesn't follow through.
- **Tips:** Combine with volume indicators to validate a breakout's strength and avoid chasing if the price has already surged too far (Chen, 2020).

News Trading

- **How it works:** News traders buy or sell based on major news events, like earnings reports or economic data. Imagine a crowded theater where everyone's reacting to a sudden announcement: The first to respond often benefit the most.

- **Risks:** Market reaction to the news is unpredictable and quick decision-making is essential.
- **Tips:** Track a real-time news feed and use smaller position sizes to minimize risk until the direction is clear (*News Trading Strategies*, n.d.).

Time-Based Trading Strategies

When you trade is as important as *how* you trade. The market has its rhythm, with certain times offering more opportunities than others.

The Best Times for Day Trading: Knowing Your Market's "Rush Hours"

- **Optimal times:** Most activity occurs in the first two hours after the market opens and the last hour before it closes. These periods are like a rush-hour commute—everyone's active, creating more price movement.
- **Tips:** Focus on high-volatility assets during these times, as they offer better chances for quick trades.

Here are some time-based strategies to help you optimize your timing and make every minute count (Dux, 2022):

The 5-Minute Trading Strategy

- **How it works:** Traders make quick trades based on 5-minute chart patterns. It's like sprinting instead of running a marathon, aiming for rapid, small gains.

- **Risks:** Fast time frames can lead to more "noise" or false signals.
- **Tips:** Use momentum indicators like the MACD or RSI to confirm direction, and don't overtrade—it's best to stick to a few well-chosen moves (Lien, 2024).

Scale-In Strategy

- **How it works:** Instead of entering with one large trade, you make multiple smaller trades over time, building up your position gradually, like planting seeds in a garden one by one rather than all at once.
- **Risks:** A change in market direction could result in accumulated small losses.
- **Tips:** Use scale-in entries during quieter times when the market is steady to avoid big swings.

The 1-Hour Trading Strategy

- **How it works:** For traders who want a broader view, the 1-hour strategy involves observing hourly charts to identify price trends. It's like watching the tide come in and go out rather than chasing individual waves.
- **Risks:** A lot of patience is required, and sudden moves can catch you off guard.
- **Tips:** Use trend indicators, like moving averages, to confirm entries and avoid over-leveraging since trades tend to be open longer (Tristan, 2023).

Session-to-Session Price Flow

- **How it works:** This looks at how prices flow between global trading sessions (Asia, Europe, and the U.S.), capturing the market's natural rhythm. Like following the sun as it rises and sets across time zones.
- **Risks:** Overnight events or early session changes can shift trends unexpectedly.
- **Tips:** Keep an eye on overlap times, like when the U.S. and European markets are both open, as this tends to bring higher volume and more reliable moves.

The Last 5 Minutes of the Hour

- **How it works:** Trading at the end of each hour capitalizes on traders closing positions, often creating brief surges. It's like timing the last sprint before a race finishes.
- **Risks:** High volatility in the final minutes can be unpredictable.
- **Tips:** Use smaller trades and focus on stocks that show clear price movement throughout the hour to avoid false signals.

Opening Minutes Analysis

- **How it works:** This approach looks for trends in the first 15–30 minutes of the trading day, catching initial market reactions. It's like the morning rush: quick, intense, and full of momentum.

- **Risks:** Sudden volatility makes it risky for beginners.
- **Tips:** Use small positions to test early trends and switch to larger trades once patterns stabilize (*Three Great Reversal Strategies for All Timeframes*, 2023).

Building a Trading Journal

Trading without a journal feels directionless and random. Your journal serves as your road map. By logging what you've done, you're creating a resource to understand what worked, what didn't, and why. It's like a diary, but one that's less about feelings and more about refining your edge in the market.

How to Create a Trading Journal Step-by-Step

Setting up a trading journal doesn't have to be complicated. Here's a step-by-step guide to help you build one that is easy to use and can be insightful.

Choose Your Medium: Book or Spreadsheet?

- **Book:** Some traders prefer the tactile nature of a book. Writing by hand can help you think through your trades more thoroughly, and a physical book feels a bit like keeping a personal diary. You can even decorate it or create categories for each page to personalize it.
- **Spreadsheet:** Spreadsheets are the digital approach and are popular for a reason. They allow for more accessible organization, data sorting, and analysis. Plus, if you're into metrics, you can include formulas for average profit, win rate, and draw down.

If you're a beginner, start with a simple notebook or digital document. You can always switch to a spreadsheet as you become more comfortable and start wanting deeper analysis (*How to Create and Maintain a Trading Journal*, 2022).

Record Every Trade Immediately

- After placing a trade, jot down the entry and exit points, stop loss, take profit, position size, and timeframe. Think of this as capturing the ingredients of your trade recipe.
- Once the trade is complete, record the outcome (win, loss, or break even) and include additional notes about what happened during the trade. For example, "Market reversed unexpectedly after a news release" or "Exited early due to nerves."

The key is to record details while they're fresh. If you wait too long, you'll likely forget important information or remember it inaccurately.

Reflect and Compile at Regular Intervals

At the end of each day, week, or month (choose whatever frequency suits you), browse your journal and look for patterns or insights.

Summarize your observations, noting things like the following:

- **Common errors:** Did you jump in too soon or move your stop loss out of fear?
- **Wins and strengths:** What setups worked best? Was there a time of day that was consistently profitable?

This reflection phase is where your journal shines. By compiling and analyzing your trades, you can see if there's something you should repeat, improve, or avoid.

Different Journal Formats: Examples to Get You Started

Your journal doesn't have to follow a rigid format; it can be as simple or detailed as you'd like. Here are a few different formats to help you get started:

Basic Journal: Just the Essentials

- **Format:** A straightforward log of each trade's basics, like entry, exit, position size, and notes.
- **Ideal Users:** Beginners or traders who want a low-maintenance option.

Comprehensive Journal: The All-In-One

- **Format:** Includes all the essentials, plus sections for trade rationale, emotional state, and post-trade review.
- **Ideal Users:** Experienced traders looking to dive deep into the psychology and analysis behind each trade.

Chart-Based Journal: Visual Approach

- **Format:** Uses screenshots of charts showing trade entry and exit points, with comments about each trade.
- **Ideal Users:** Visual learners who find patterns easier to spot when seeing the charts alongside their notes.

Data-Driven Journal: The Metric Tracker

- **Format:** A spreadsheet with metrics like win rate, average profit/loss, and monthly profit.
- **Ideal Users:** Traders who enjoy quantitative analysis and want to track their performance over time.

Choose a format that feels right for you. Many traders start with a basic approach and add complexity as they gain experience.

A 15-Minute Forex Trading Strategy to Add to Your Journal

To kick-start your journal, here's a 15-minute forex trading strategy. This simple setup is ideal for quick trades, giving you ample material to record and reflect on.

The 15-Minute Momentum Strategy

1. **Setup:** Use a 15-minute chart and a momentum indicator (like MACD).
2. **Entry:** Look for the MACD to cross above the zero line (for a buy) or below the zero line (for a sell).
3. **Stop loss:** Place your stop loss below the most recent support level for a buy or above the recent resistance level for a sell.
4. **Take profit:** Aim for a 1:1 or 2:1 risk-reward ratio, exiting the trade once the price moves in your favor.
5. **Record and review:** Once you finish the trade, write down the entry, exit, and profit/loss, along with notes on the market context (like news or major events).

Keeping a trading journal is like being both the player and coach. The more details you add, the better you can learn from each trade. The insights and patterns you'll discover will help you fine-tune your approach, making you a more skilled and self-aware trader.

EIGHT

Lessons From the Titans

Learn every day, but especially from the experiences of others. It's cheaper!

John C. Bogle

Old Is Gold

Trading is like stepping into an intricate maze that seasoned traders have mapped out through years of navigating ups, downs, and unexpected twists. You can shorten your learning curve by learning from their successes and failures. You can also gear up with tools, strategies, and insights to help you improve your approach.

For example, sports teams analyze past games to improve their performance, and successful traders regularly analyze past trades. Think of each trade as a lesson. When you take the time to examine each outcome, you're learning without risking capital in real-time. In a way, your past trades become your personal *textbook on* trading.

Importance of Analyzing Past Trades

1. **Identifying patterns:** Spotting patterns over time reveals your strengths and weaknesses. Are there certain types of trades where you're consistently profitable or situations where you tend to make hasty decisions?
2. **Refining strategies:** Reviewing trades shows which strategies work for you versus ones you might need to tweak or abandon.
3. **Managing emotions:** Emotions can be your biggest obstacle in trading. By revisiting your past trades, you're forced to confront moments where emotion—fear, greed, impatience—might've led to a loss, helping you build the discipline to make logical,

level-headed decisions in the future (*Learning from Experience*, 2023).

Types of Trades You Must Analyze

Not every trade will teach you something profound, but essential experiences, especially major wins and losses, provide invaluable insights. Here's a quick guide on which trades to focus on:

1. **Winning trades:** Successful trades are worth revisiting to pinpoint what went right. Were market conditions particularly favorable? Did you enter at the perfect moment, or was it a stroke of luck? When you understand the mechanics behind these trades, you can replicate that success.
2. **Losing trades:** Losses sting, but they're good learning opportunities. Examining losing trades reveals if you were too impulsive or took on too much risk. Losses show you which parts of your strategy need refining or where you might need to rethink your approach.
3. **Trades you felt conflicted about:** Trades that felt uncertain or were based on a *hunch* rather than solid analysis are also worth reviewing. These trades might highlight a need to improve your research process or reinforce that gut instincts alone aren't always reliable.
4. **Trades in unfamiliar markets:** Trading outside your comfort zone or in a new market can highlight gaps in your knowledge or areas where further study might benefit.

Elements to Analyze in Past Trades

1. **Entry and exit points:** Consider when you decide to enter and exit the trade. Ask yourself whether you entered too soon or too late or were holding on too long in the hopes of more significant gains. This review shows whether you're following your strategy or letting impulses take over.
2. **Market conditions:** Was the market trending, stable, or volatile? Context matters, as certain strategies work better under specific conditions. Knowing what conditions played into your wins or losses can guide you on when to use specific techniques.
3. **Your emotional state:** Did you feel confident, anxious, or impulsive during this trade? Emotional cues, while not quantifiable, play a massive role in outcomes. Keeping a note of your emotions during a trade can help you spot when they might be influencing your decisions too heavily.
4. **Trade duration:** Sometimes, the length of time for which you hold a trade impacts its success. Reviewing how long you held each trade might help you recognize that certain time frames work better with your strategy or that you tend to abandon trades too soon.
5. **Market analysis accuracy:** Review whether your initial predictions matched the market's behavior. Were you able to foresee trends, or did the market go in a different direction than you expected? Understanding how accurate your market analysis was can help you improve future analyses.

How to Get the Most out of Your Analysis

1. **Create a trade journal:** Record details about each trade, including entry and exit points, market conditions, and your emotional state. This journal is a reference guide that helps you track your growth and recurring challenges.
2. **Highlight patterns and trends:** After a few entries, start looking for patterns. If you notice that trades executed at a particular time of day or under certain market conditions tend to succeed, take note. Similarly, you'll know what to avoid if certain trade types or emotions consistently lead to losses.
3. **Set improvement goals:** Based on your findings, create specific goals. These include reducing impulsive trades, improving accuracy in predicting trends, or holding trades longer in certain situations.

4. **Seek feedback from experienced traders:** It can also be helpful to discuss your findings with other traders or mentors who can provide a fresh perspective or offer advice on refining your strategies.

Profiles of Day Trading Titans

Learning from masters in any field is a game-changer. Many legendary traders have carved their paths with a blend of innovation, timing, and sheer tenacity. Here's a look at a few titans:

1. **Paul Tudor Jones:** Known for his foresight in predicting market crashes, Jones emphasizes disciplined risk management. His strategy revolves around knowing when to step back and avoiding significant losses during risky periods.
2. **George Soros:** Famous for "Breaking the Bank of England," Soros' approach involves making bold moves when he has a high level of conviction. He's a reminder that, sometimes, success requires you to take calculated risks and have the courage to act decisively.
3. **Jesse Livermore:** A pioneer of short-selling, Livermore mastered the art of market timing. His journey shows the importance of observing market trends closely and trusting your research.
4. **Linda Bradford Raschke:** An accomplished trader who focuses on day trading and swing trading, Raschke is known for her disciplined, data-driven

approach. Her story shows the power of consistency and learning from experience.

Each of these traders has a unique philosophy, and by learning from them, you can incorporate their insights into your strategy and adapt their successful practices to your style (Blystone, 2024).

Against the Odds: A Trader's Remarkable One-Year Journey to Success

Success in trading often feels elusive, something that takes years to achieve. But some stories remind us that, with dedication, discipline, and a touch of resilience, life can change in a short time. Meet Jack, a young trader who started with no experience but, in just one year, transformed his financial life entirely. Jack's story is a testament to what's possible with the right mindset and effort.

Jack's Starting Point

Jack was in his late twenties and had a steady job in customer support, but he found himself feeling unfulfilled and financially stagnant. Aware that his 9-to-5 job wasn't leading him to the financial independence he craved, he began researching alternative ways to create wealth. Trading piqued his interest. Though risky, he knew it offered the potential for quick returns with the right approach. Driven by curiosity and ambition, he decided to jump in.

Step 1: The Learning Phase

Jack knew he couldn't rely on luck alone. His first step was educating himself rigorously. In the evenings, he spent hours watching trading tutorials, reading articles, and devouring books on trading strategies and market psychology. He also signed up for a mentor program, where he learned about risk management, setting realistic goals, and controlling emotional responses.

Step 2: Practicing in the Safety of Simulated Trading

He treated this phase as if he were back in school, dedicating his evenings and weekends to learning everything he could. He experimented with various strategies and observed how the markets behaved during different times and events. He even took notes to document what worked and what didn't, a habit that later proved invaluable. He did this for 3 months.

With a solid foundation of knowledge, he started paper trading. This let him practice without the risk of real financial loss. It felt different from reading theory because he could see his strategies in action. He realized that some approaches that seemed foolproof in theory didn't work as expected. However, this period allowed him to refine his methods and adapt his strategies before putting real money on the line.

Step 3: The Transition to Live Trading

After a few months of simulated trading, he felt confident enough to enter the market. He set aside a modest sum, just $1,000, and took a disciplined approach to his trades. He adhered strictly to a 1% risk-per-trade rule, meaning he never risked more than 1% of his capital on a single trade, which kept his losses minimal. He also set strict stop-loss and take-profit levels to keep his trades within his risk tolerance.

Step 4: Facing Setbacks

Despite his preparations, his journey wasn't entirely smooth. In the first few weeks, he faced multiple small losses. There were moments when he questioned if trading was for him, but he reminded himself that every successful trader experiences setbacks. Learning from these losses, he tweaked his strategy and focused on keeping his emotions in check.

Step 5: Building Momentum

To maintain perspective, Jack kept a trading journal. This helped him identify patterns in the market and his responses. Slowly, he began to understand that his mistakes often resulted from emotional decisions or a deviation from his strategy. As he worked on his discipline, his trades began to show a small but consistent profit.

After six months, he noticed that his profits were beginning to exceed his losses. While his gains weren't huge, they were consistent, and he was steadily growing his account balance. As he gained confidence, he increased his capital to $5,000, reinvesting his profits along the way.

His turning point came when he found a strategy that worked well for him: Trading around specific market events. He realized he had a knack for interpreting the market's response to economic news, like interest rate announcements or quarterly earnings reports. By honing in on this edge, he achieved a higher win rate. He focused on perfecting his niche approach rather than getting caught up in every trend.

Step 6: Hitting His One-Year Goal

As the one-year mark approached, his bank balance had grown significantly. By compounding his gains, he turned his initial $1,000 investment into nearly $25,000—a staggering growth rate far exceeding his expectations. Jack's journey wasn't solely about financial gain; it also built his confidence, discipline, and resilience.

While many new traders focus solely on money, Jack attributes his success to his growth mindset. Instead of becoming discouraged by losses, he used them as stepping stones to develop more robust, more reliable strategies.

Lessons From Jack's Journey

1. **Educate yourself thoroughly:** Jack's dedication to learning before he started trading was a key factor in his success. The market rewards those who understand it.
2. **Practice before going live:** Paper trading gave him the safe space he needed to refine his strategies. It was like training wheels for the market, allowing him to build confidence without the risk of loss.

3. **Set clear rules and stick to them:** Jack's adherence to his risk management rules kept him from losing too much too quickly. Consistent success comes from controlled, disciplined actions.
4. **Keep a trading journal:** He tracked his decisions and emotional state, and he was able to identify patterns and improve over time.
5. **Find your edge:** Jack's success took off when he found a strategy that aligned with his strengths: Trading around market events. Finding and perfecting your niche is a game-changer.
6. **Persistence pays off:** Success in trading isn't guaranteed, but perseverance and resilience are invaluable. Jack's setbacks didn't deter him; they motivated him to keep improving.

While trading isn't a guaranteed path to riches, it offers the potential for life-changing gains when approached with discipline and commitment. With a strong foundation, consistent practice, and a bit of self-belief, you can make strides in a short time. It's not about beating the market; it's about steadily improving and achieving personal growth along the way.

Jack's one-year journey proves that, against the odds, quick success in trading is possible for those who are willing to learn, adapt, and stay the course (*From Rags to Riches*, 2023).

Conclusion

As you prepare to step in, remember that this is just the beginning of an exciting and sometimes challenging but ultimately rewarding journey. Trading takes time to master, and while the information you've absorbed may feel vast and intricate, know that with practice and patience, the concepts and strategies outlined here will soon become second nature.

Every chart, every indicator, and every trade you make brings you closer to the confidence and proficiency needed to thrive in this fast-paced arena.

Let this book be your trusted guide, a resource you can turn to time and again. Revisit the chapters that delve into risk management, market psychology, and strategic planning whenever you need a refresher. With each read, you'll uncover new insights and solidify the foundation of knowledge you need to make sound decisions. The path to success is often paved by those willing to learn, grow, and most importantly, persevere.

But remember, the market is constantly evolving. New trends emerge, technologies advance, and strategies are refined over time. To stay on top, you must be a lifelong learner, committed to honing your skills and staying updated with the latest innovations and trends. The best traders embrace change and are always willing to adapt and integrate new techniques into their practice.

As you gain experience, you'll start to see patterns, and certain aspects of trading will become more intuitive. The research, the risk calculations, and the moment-to-moment decision-making will feel less daunting. Yet, no matter how skilled you become, always approach the market with humility. Even the most experienced traders encounter challenges and learn new lessons.

If you ever find yourself uncertain, let that be an opportunity to deepen your understanding. Seek additional resources, participate in trader communities, and don't hesitate to ask questions or revisit fundamentals. Your growth as a trader will be shaped not only by the knowledge you acquire but also by your willingness to explore beyond the pages of this book.

Ultimately, trading is more than just a way to profit; it's a journey of self-discovery, discipline, and resilience. You're not just learning how to make trades but building a mindset that can handle the market's ups and downs with confidence and composure. Stay curious, disciplined, and, above all, committed to your progress.

As you turn this last page, know you're stepping into a world filled with potential. While this can be your guide and road map, real growth comes from what you experience firsthand.

Welcome to the journey of day trading mastery—may this book serve as your foundation and may you find success, not just in numbers but in the knowledge, skills, and self-assurance you build along the way.

Now that you have everything you need to start trading with confidence and building the financial freedom you've been dreaming of, it's time to share your experience and help others find the same support.

By leaving your honest opinion of this book on Amazon, you'll show other aspiring traders where they can find clear, actionable strategies to begin their day trading journey. Your words can inspire someone to take the first step toward mastering the markets and achieving their financial goals.

Thank you for your help. The art and science of day trading thrive when we share what we've learned with others—and you're helping keep that spirit alive.

Ready to make a difference? Share your review below

Your feedback means the world to me—and it just might change the world for someone else.

With gratitude,

Daniel Fernell

Glossary

The following is a list of the trading terms used in this book along with their meanings (*Glossary of Trading Terms*, n.d.).

A

- **Ask price:** The price at which a trader can buy a currency pair. It's usually higher than the bid price.
- **Asset:** Anything that holds value and can be traded, such as currencies, commodities, stocks, and bonds.

B

- **Bar chart:** A chart that displays detailed information on price movements within a specified period. Each bar represents one period (such as a minute, hour, or day.) and shows the opening, high, low, and closing prices for that period.

- **Bid price:** The price at which a trader can sell a currency pair.
- **Broker:** An intermediary who executes trades on behalf of traders, offering access to trading platforms.

C

- **Candlestick chart:** A chart showing the high, low, open, and close prices of a currency within a specific time frame, used to predict future price movements.
- **Contract for difference or CFD:** A financial derivative that allows traders to speculate on the price movement of assets without actually owning them.
- **Currency pair:** The two currencies being traded, where the first is the base currency and the second is the quote currency (e.g., EUR/USD).

D

- **Day trading:** A trading style where all positions are opened and closed within the same trading day.
- **Drawdown:** A peak-to-trough decline during a specific period, usually expressed as a percentage.

E

- **Economic indicators:** Statistics released by governments or organizations that provide insight into economic performance, such as GDP, employment rates, or inflation.
- **Exchange rate:** The rate at which one currency can be exchanged for another.

F

- **Fibonacci retracement:** A technical analysis tool used to identify potential support and resistance levels based on the Fibonacci sequence.
- **Foreign exchange or Forex:** The global marketplace for trading national currencies against one another.

G

- **Going long or buying long:** Buying a currency pair with the expectation that its price will rise.
- **Going short or selling short:** Selling a currency pair with the expectation that its price will fall.

H

- **Hedging:** A strategy to offset potential losses by taking a position in a related asset.

- **High-frequency trading or HFT:** A trading strategy that uses algorithms to execute a large number of trades in fractions of a second.

I

- **Indicator:** A statistical measurement or tool used in technical analysis to predict future price movements.
- **Interest rate:** The rate charged by a central bank on loans to commercial banks, which can affect currency value.

K

- **Key level:** Important price levels that act as major support or resistance, such as round numbers (e.g., 1.3,000 in EUR/USD).

L

- **Leverage:** Using borrowed funds to amplify potential returns, allowing traders to control larger positions than their actual investment.
- **Line chart:** A chart used to represent the movement of currency prices over time. It connects closing prices for a specific currency pair with a continuous line, providing a straightforward visual representation of price trends.

- **Liquidity:** The ease with which an asset can be bought or sold in the market without affecting its price.

M

- **Margin:** The amount of money required in a trader's account to open and maintain a leveraged position.
- **Margin call:** A demand from a broker for additional funds to maintain a position that has moved against the trader.
- **Market order:** An order to buy or sell immediately at the current market price.

N

- **Net position:** The amount of currency held, which can be either long or short.

O

- **Over-the-counter or OTC markets:** A decentralized market where forex trading happens directly between two parties without a central exchange.
- **Overbought/Oversold:** Conditions indicating that a currency may be overvalued (overbought) or undervalued (oversold), often leading to a reversal.

P

- **Percentage in point or Pip:** The smallest price move in a currency pair, usually the fourth decimal place in most pairs (e.g., 0.0001).
- **Position:** The amount of currency a trader holds, which can be long (buy) or short (sell).
- **Price action:** The movement of a currency's price over time, used in technical analysis.

R

- **Resistance level:** A price level where a currency pair struggles to rise above, often seen as a point to sell.
- **Risk management:** Identifying and managing potential risks in trading, including setting stop losses and position sizing.

S

- **Scalping:** A trading style involving multiple quick daily trades to gain small profits from small price movements.
- **Spread:** The difference between the bid and ask price represents a trade's cost.
- **Stop-loss order:** An order to automatically close a trade if the price moves against the trader by a specified amount, limiting potential loss.

- **Support level:** A price level where a currency pair tends to find buying interest, often seen as a point to buy.

T

- **Take-profit order:** An order that closes a trade once a currency reaches a specific profit level, securing gains.
- **Technical analysis:** A method focusing on historical price data and chart patterns to predict future movements.
- **Trailing stop:** A stop-loss order that automatically adjusts as the trade moves in the trader's favor, protecting gains while allowing for further upside.
- **Trend:** The general direction of the market over a specific period, which can be up, down, or sideways.

U

- **Underlying asset:** The actual asset being traded, like a currency in the forex market.

V

- **Volatility:** The degree of price fluctuation in a currency pair over time; high volatility presents both risk and opportunity.

W

- **Win rate:** The percentage of trades that end in profit, a critical factor in assessing the effectiveness of a trading strategy.

Y

- **Yield:** The earnings generated and realized on an investment, often used in reference to bonds and other fixed-income securities but also applicable to forex.

References

Anderson, J. (2018, July 24). *Your essential guide to day trading: Rules, tips, and strategies*. GOBankingRates. https://www.gobankingrates.com/investing/stocks/day-trading-rules/

Bajaj Finserv. (2023). *Paper trading*. BajajFinserv. https://www.bajajfinserv.in/paper-trading

Bajpai, P. (2024, May 9). *What to know about day trading as a beginner*. Investopedia. https://www.investopedia.com/articles/active-trading/071414/day-trading-rules-rookies-dont-play-it-ear.asp

Balancing risk and reward. (2019). IG. https://www.ig.com/en/ig-academy/money-management/balancing-risk-and-reward

Baldridge, R. (2023, May 8). *What is your risk tolerance?* Forbes. https://www.forbes.com/advisor/investing/what-is-your-risk-tolerance/

Barone, A. (2021, August 5). *Introduction to momentum trading*. Investopedia. https://www.investopedia.com/trading/introduction-to-momentum-trading/

Bechard, L. (2024, May 17). *Day trading computer setup and equipment*. Bullish Bears. https://bullishbears.com/day-trading-computer-setup/

Beers, B. (2019). *How to pick a broker*. Investopedia. https://www.investopedia.com/articles/younginvestors/06/firstbroker.asp

Beginners guide to investing in bonds. (n.d.). SC. https://www.sc.com/ke/investments/learn/understanding-bonds-for-beginners/

A beginner's guide to trading crypto. (2023, November 12). Wirex. https://wirexapp.com/blog/post/a-beginners-guide-to-trading-crypto-0757

Best day trading trading strategies explained. (n.d.). Tradeciety. https://tradeciety.com/best-day-trading-trading-strategies-explained

Best trading quotes - 15 trading tips from the best traders. (2023, March 29). Tradeciety; Quantum Trade Solutions GmbH. https://tradeciety.com/trading-quotes

Blystone, D. (2024, March 3). *The world's 10 most famous traders of all time*. Investopedia. https://www.investopedia.com/articles/active-trading/041515/worlds-10-most-famous-traders-all-time.asp

Bogle, J., C. (2024). *John C. Bogle quote: "Learn every day, but especially from the experiences of others. it's cheaper!"* Quotefancy. https://quotefancy.com/

quote/1583954/John-C-Bogle-Learn-every-day-but-especially-from-the-experiences-of-others-It-s-cheaper

BrainyQuote. (2024). BrainyQuote. https://www.brainyquote.com/topics/mitigate-quotes

Broking, G. (2023, June 7). *How to choose the right brokerage firm for your trading needs...?* LinkedIn. https://www.linkedin.com/pulse/how-choose-right-brokerage-firm-your-trading-needs-gill-broking/

Cameron, R. (2014, June 24). *Day trading rules for beginners*. Warrior Trading. https://www.warriortrading.com/day-trading-rules/

Cameron, R. (2015, June 10). *How to use hotkeys for day trading*. Warrior Trading. https://www.warriortrading.com/hot-key-video-lesson/

Cameron, R. (2021, November 20). *Momentum day trading strategies for beginners: A step by step guide*. Warrior Trading. https://www.warriortrading.com/momentum-day-trading-strategy/

Cameron, R. (2022, May 26). *Reversal day trading strategies*. Warrior Trading. https://www.warriortrading.com/reversal-trading-strategy/

Capre, C. (2012, April 23). *Engulfing candle - the truth no one is telling you*. 2nd Skies Trading. https://2ndskiesforex.com/forex-strategies/engulfing-bars-the-truth-no-one-is-telling-you/

Carey, T. W. (2024, August 8). *Top technical analysis tools for traders*. Investopedia. https://www.investopedia.com/articles/active-trading/121014/best-technical-analysis-trading-software.asp

Carlson, D. (2020, May 7). *The ultimate guide to bonds*. US News & World Report; U.S. News & World Report. https://money.usnews.com/investing/investing-101/articles/the-ultimate-guide-to-bonds

Chen, J. (2019). *What is investment position sizing?* Investopedia. https://www.investopedia.com/terms/p/positionsizing.asp

Chen, J. (2020). *The anatomy of trading breakouts*. Investopedia. https://www.investopedia.com/articles/trading/08/trading-breakouts.asp

Chen, J. (2021, August 25). *High-Frequency trading - HFT*. Investopedia. https://www.investopedia.com/terms/h/high-frequency-trading.asp

Chen, T. (2023, August 2). *How to join a trading community in 2023 (step-by-step tutorial)*. HowToTrade. https://howtotrade.com/blog/how-to-join-trading-community/

Christina, B. (2022, April 6). *What is real-time market data & how to use it*. Intrinio. https://intrinio.com/blog/what-is-real-time-market-data-how-to-use-it

Churchill, W. (2015). *TOP 25 strategic quotes (of 380)*. A-Z Quotes. https://www.azquotes.com/quotes/topics/strategic.html#google_vignette

Cobra Trading, Inc. (2022, February 7). *Trading with hot keys best practices | cobra trading*. Cobra Trading. https://www.cobratrading.com/blog/hot-keys-day-trading/

Commodities trading. (n.d.). Capital. https://capital.com/trade-commodities

Coulcher, Z. (2020, March 5). *Ten quotes about tools to inspire greatness*. Defiance Tools. https://www.defiancetools.com/blogs/guides/ten-quotes-about-tools-to-inspire-greatness

Cutkovic, M. (n.d.). *What is a breakout trading strategy & how to trade it?* Axi. https://www.axi.com/int/blog/education/breakout-trading-strategy

Davis, C. (2024, August 26). *How to invest in stocks: A step-by-step for beginners*. NerdWallet. https://www.nerdwallet.com/article/investing/how-to-invest-in-stocks

Day in the life of a day trader | how to successfully day trade. (2022, March 4). Bookmap. https://bookmap.com/blog/a-day-in-the-life-of-a-day-trader

Day trading terminology: The top terms every trader should know! (n.d.). Warrior Trading. https://www.warriortrading.com/day-trading-terminology/

Deer, M. (2023). *How to trade cryptocurrency: A step-by-step crypto trading guide*. Cointelegraph. https://cointelegraph.com/learn/how-to-trade-cryptocurrencies-the-ultimate-beginners-guide

Determining where to set your stop-loss. (2023, June 4). Investopedia. https://www.investopedia.com/ask/answers/030915/how-do-i-determine-where-set-my-stop-loss.asp

Don't fall for these common myths about day trading. (2021, January 27). Traders Accounting. https://tradersaccounting.com/2021/01/27/dont-fall-for-these-common-myths-about-day-trading/

Dr. Pipslow. (2022, June). *3 tips to help you develop self-discipline in trading*. Babypips. https://www.babypips.com/trading/forex-3-tips-to-develop-self-discipline-2022-06-01

Dr. Pipslow. (2023, June 2). *5 exit strategies to consider in each trading setup*. Babypips. https://www.babypips.com/trading/5-exit-strategies-consider-setup-2023-06-02

Dux, S. (2022, March 9). *When is the best time to make trades?* LinkedIn. https://www.linkedin.com/pulse/when-best-time-make-trades-you-day-trading-xiuxian-du-steven-dux--1f/

Elopre, J. L. (2023, July 21). *Strategies to mitigate risks in international trade and compliance*. Proventa International. https://proventainternational.com/strategies-to-mitigate-risks-in-international-trade-and-compliance/

ETFs for beginners. (2023). JustETF. https://www.justetf.com/en/academy/etf-for-beginners.html#intro

Everything you need to know about automated crypto trading bot. (2021). Dev Technosys. https://devtechnosys.com/guide/automated-crypto-trading-bot.php

Everything you need to know about bonds. (n.d.). Pacific Investment Management Company LLC. https://www.pimco.com/eu/en/resources/education/everything-you-need-to-know-about-bonds

Farley, A. (2023, April 7). *Pros and cons of paper trading.* Investopedia. https://www.investopedia.com/articles/active-trading/072915/pros-and-cons-paper-trading.asp

Farley, A. (2022, February 8). *Simple and effective exit trading strategies.* Investopedia. https://www.investopedia.com/articles/active-trading/020915/mustknow-simple-effective-exit-trading-strategies.asp

Five advantages of being a day trader. (2021, June 3). Traders Accounting. https://tradersaccounting.com/2021/06/03/five-advantages-of-being-a-day-trader/

Folger, J. (2023, July 3). *Best online brokers and trading platforms January 2024.* Time. https://time.com/personal-finance/article/best-online-brokers/

Fontinelle, E. (2023, September 29). *4 basic things to know about bonds.* Investopedia. https://www.investopedia.com/articles/bonds/08/bond-market-basics.asp

Fox, S. (2022, October 4). *Unknown dangers: The risks of day trading.* Ridgewood Investments. https://ridgewoodinvestments.com/day-trading-risks

Frankel, M. (n.d.). *How to invest in ETFs.* The Motley Fool. https://www.fool.com/investing/how-to-invest/etfs/

Friedberg, B. (2017, July 14). *The 5 best day trading strategies.* GOBankingRates. https://www.gobankingrates.com/investing/stocks/day-trading-strategies/

From rags to riches: A day trader's tale of fortunes and foresight. (2023, June 23). BOSS Magazine. https://thebossmagazine.com/day-traders-fortune-foresight/

Fuller, N. (2018, February 2). *Before you place your next trade, ask yourself these 10 questions.* Learn to Trade the Market. https://www.learntotradethemarket.com/forex-trading-strategies/place-trade-ask-10-questions

Fullerton, G. (2019). *What are the advantages of using a broker over an exchange when trading stocks?* Quora. https://www.quora.com/What-are-the-advantages-of-using-a-broker-over-an-exchange-when-trading-stocks

Fundamental analysis tools: Top tools for investors. (n.d.). Angel One. https://

www.angelone.in/knowledge-center/share-market/fundamental-analy sis-tools

Gilbertson, S. (2024, January 22). *11 ways to upgrade your wi-fi and make your internet faster*. Wired. https://www.wired.com/story/how-to-make-your-wifi-better-faster/

Glossary of trading terms. (n.d.). IG. https://www.ig.com/uk/glossary-trad ing-terms

Graham, B. (n.d.). *7 criteria for selecting value stocks*. Winvesta. https://www.winvesta.in/blog/benjamin-grahams-seven-criteria-selecting-value-stocks

Groette, O. (2024a, March 10). *Trend following trading strategies and systems (backtest results) - quantified strategies*. Quantified Strategies. https://www.quantifiedstrategies.com/trend-following-trading-strategy/

Groette, O. (2024b, June 17). *Scale-In trading strategy: Overview, rules, backtest analysis - quantifiedstrategies.com*. Quantified Strategies. https://www.quantifiedstrategies.com/scale-in-trading-strategy/

Guide to 6 day trading tools (plus important skills). (2024). Indeed Career Guide. https://www.indeed.com/career-advice/career-development/day-trading-tools

Guide to commodity trading secrets. (2024, May 26). Corporate Finance Institute. https://corporatefinanceinstitute.com/resources/commodities/a-guide-to-commodity-trading-secrets/

Hayes, A. (2021, April 29). *Introduction to technical analysis price patterns*. Investopedia. https://www.investopedia.com/articles/technical/112601.asp

Hayes, A. (2022, March 14). *Technical analysis: What it is and how to use it in investing*. Investopedia. https://www.investopedia.com/terms/t/techni calanalysis.asp

Herrity, J. (2024). *107 quotes to motivate you throughout your workday*. Indeed Career Guide. https://www.indeed.com/career-advice/career-develop ment/quotes-to-motivate-workers

Hickmann, S. (2023, November 21). *Position sizing for risk management*. Medium; STRIDE.trade. https://medium.com/stride-trade/position-sizing-for-risk-management-be294b796117

Horton, M. (2019). *Common examples of risk management*. Investopedia. https://www.investopedia.com/ask/answers/050715/what-are-some-examples-risk-management-techniques.asp

Hot keys - the ultimate guide for day traders. (2020, September 24). CenterPoint Securities. https://centerpointsecurities.com/hot-keys/

How do you set and track trading goals? (2023, August 21). LinkedIn. https://www.linkedin.com/advice/3/how-do-you-set-track-trading-goals-skills-technical-analysis

How emergency funds are important for a forex trader. (2023, November 10). Forex GDP. https://www.forexgdp.com/learn/emergency-funds-importance/

How important is the internet performance on trading? (2022, December 11). NewsnReleases. https://newsnreleases.com/2022/12/11/how-important-is-the-internet-performance-on-trading/

How to balance the risk and reward of an option strategy? (2024, February 22). Moomoo. https://www.moomoo.com/us/learn/detail-how-to-balance-the-risk-and-reward-of-an-option-strategy-116925-231104055

How to be a successful trader? Tips to improve your trading mindset. (2024). Fbs. https://fbs.com/blog/how-to-be-a-successful-trader-tips-to-improve-your-trading-mindset-342

How to build a crypto trading bot in 2023: Complete guide. (2023, May 11). LinkedIn. https://www.linkedin.com/pulse/how-build-crypto-trading-bot-2023-complete-guide-strivemindz/

How to change a life in one year: A trader's success story. (2021, July 10). Forexlive. https://www.forexlive.com/Education/

How to control emotions while trading - strategies and techniques. (2023, April 4). The5ers Forex Prop Firm. https://the5ers.com/how-to-control-emotions-while-trading/

How to create a successful trading plan. (n.d.). IG. https://www.ig.com/en/trading-strategies/how-to-create-a-successful-trading-plan-181210

How to create an excellent and performing day trading plan. (2022, May 13). Real Trading. https://realtrading.com/trading-blog/day-trading-plan/

How to create and maintain a trading journal: A step by step guide. (2022, September 16). Medium; Coinmonks. https://medium.com/coinmonks/how-to-create-and-maintain-a-trading-journal-a-step-by-step-guide-a041c68f148f

How to find the best risk and reward ratio in FX. (2023, November 19). Axiory. https://www.axiory.com/trading-resources/risk-management/risk-reward-ratio

How to manage the emotions of trading. (2022, December 22). IG. https://www.ig.com/en/master-your-trading-mind/managing-emotions/how-to-manage-the-emotions-of-trading

How to practise discipline in trading. (2024). FXTM. https://www.forextime.com/education/videos/how-to-practice-discipline-in-trading

How to read level 2 market data - using an order book for trading strategies. (2024, September 9). Moomoo. https://www.moomoo.com/sg/learn/detail-how-to-read-level-2-market-data-using-an-order-book-for-trading-strategies-66157-220709059

How to read stock charts and trading patterns. (2023, January 18). Schwab Brokerage. https://www.schwab.com/learn/story/how-to-read-stock-charts-and-trading-patterns

How to set realistic trading goals for your trading account. (2023, April 12). Samco; Discount Brokers in India - Samco Securities. https://www.samco.in/knowledge-center/articles/how-to-set-realistic-trading-goals/

How to set trading goals. (n.d.). CMCmarkets. https://www.cmcmarkets.com/en/trading-guides/considerations-when-defining-trading-goals

How to set up stop-loss & take-profit orders. (2024, August 2). EToro. https://www.etoro.com/trading/how-to-set-stop-loss-and-take-profit-targets/

How to trade cryptocurrencies. (n.d.). IG. https://www.ig.com/en/cryptocurrency-trading/how-to-trade-cryptocurrency

Introduction to trade execution algorithms. (2019, February 25). Blaze Portfolio. https://blazeportfolio.com/blog/introduction-to-trade-execution-algorithms-2/

Invest in global markets with a Swiss bank. (n.d.). Flowbank. https://www.flowbank.com/

Jackson, A., L. (2024, August 26). *How to read stock charts: Quick-Start guide for beginners.* NerdWallet. https://www.nerdwallet.com/article/investing/how-to-interpret-stock-charts-and-data

Keeping track of your trading performance. (2019). IG. https://www.ig.com/uk/learn-to-trade/ig-academy/tools-for-traders/important-metrics?source=dailyfx

Kokaz, A. (2020, July 3). *Trading execution algorithms - Ali Kokaz - medium.* Medium. https://ali-kokaz.medium.com/trading-execution-algorithms-17671e315bc8

Kramer, L. (2019). *Long position vs. short position: What's the difference?* Investopedia. https://www.investopedia.com/ask/answers/100314/whats-difference-between-long-and-short-position-market.asp

Kuepper, J. (2019a). *10 day trading strategies for beginners.* Investopedia. https://www.investopedia.com/articles/trading/06/daytradingretail.asp

Kuepper, J. (2019b). *An introduction to day trading.* Investopedia. https://www.investopedia.com/articles/trading/05/011705.asp

Langager, C. (2022, August 23). *A beginner's guide to stock investing.* Investopedia. https://www.investopedia.com/articles/basics/06/invest1000.asp

Learning from experience: The power of analyzing past trades to improve your trading skills. (2023). Vstar. https://www.vstar.com/article/learn-trading-from-past-experiences

Learning from experienced traders. (2023, September 28). Market Pulse. https://fxopen.com/blog/en/learning-from-experienced-traders/

Levine, S. (2024, October 30). *Seven best online brokers 2024*. StockBrokers. https://www.stockbrokers.com/guides/online-stock-brokers

Lien, K. (2024). *The 5-minute chart trading strategy*. Investopedia. https://www.investopedia.com/articles/forex/08/five-minute-momo.asp

Lioudis, N. (2019). *Commodities trading: An overview*. Investopedia. https://www.investopedia.com/investing/commodities-trading-overview/

Lund, B. (n.d.). *Trading psychology: Mastering your emotions and instincts for successful trading*. Britannica. https://www.britannica.com/money/trading-psychology

Majaski, C. (2020, June 10). *The difference between day trading and swing trading*. Investopedia. https://www.investopedia.com/articles/active-trading/052815/pros-cons-day-trading-vs-swing-trading.asp

McBride, G. (2024, January 29). *What is risk tolerance and why is it important?* Bankrate. https://www.bankrate.com/investing/what-is-risk-tolerance/#rtv

Mitchell, C. (2021, March 4). *Goals for novice traders*. Investopedia. https://www.investopedia.com/articles/basics/12/goals-for-novice-traders.asp

Mitchell, C. (2014). *The engulfing candle day-trading strategy*. The Balance. https://www.thebalancemoney.com/engulfing-candle-day-trading-strategy-1030873

Mitchell, C. (2021, March 4). *Reversal*. Investopedia. https://www.investopedia.com/terms/r/reversal.asp

Mitchell, C. (2024, October 25). *Tactics for improving self-control and discipline while trading - trade that swing*. Trade That Swing. https://tradethatswing.com/tactics-for-improving-self-control-and-discipline-while-trading/

Momentum trading strategies: A beginner's guide. (n.d.). IG. https://www.ig.com/en/trading-strategies/momentum-trading-strategies--a-beginners-guide-190905

Morshed, A. (2022, October 5). *Secrets of the richest day traders*. Traders Union. https://tradersunion.com/interesting-articles/richest-forex-traders-trading-secrets-life-stories/secrets-of-the-richest-day-traders/

Most day traders end up losing money over time. here's why. (2023, January 19). Big Think. https://bigthink.com/sponsored/day-trading-reality/

Murison, S. (2019). *Strategy and planning*. IG. https://www.ig.com/uk/trad

ing-strategies?source=dailyfx

Nelson, N. (2023, May 13). *10 ways an online community of stock trader can transform your trading game - tweak your biz*. Tweak Your Biz. https://tweakyourbiz.com/posts/online-community-stock-trading-benefits

News trading strategies | how to trade the news. (n.d.). AvaTrade. https://www.avatrade.com/education/online-trading-strategies/news-trading-strategies

Nichols, A. (2010, July 1). *The benefits of using a brokerage firm*. AllBusiness. https://www.allbusiness.com/the-benefits-of-using-a-brokerage-firm-3779172-1.html

The not-so-hidden risks of day trading. (2022, June 7). Navy Federal Credit Union. https://www.navyfederal.org/makingcents/investing/risks-of-day-trading.html

Oddmund Groette. (2024, April 8). *Trading edge: What is it and how to find them*. Quantified Strategies. https://www.quantifiedstrategies.com/trading-edge/

Odion, W. (2023, November 1). *Discover day trading and swing trading*. LinkedIn. https://www.linkedin.com/pulse/day-trading-vs-swing-explained-choosing-your-path-success-odion-nu31f/

One hundred and one inspirational trading quotes and what they mean. (2021, July 23). Trading Education. https://trading-education.com/101-inspirational-trading-quotes-and-what-they-mean

Online trading courses. (2019). IG. https://www.ig.com/uk/learn-to-trade/ig-academy/courses?source=dailyfx

Palmer, B. (2022, March 17). *Institutional vs. retail investors: What's the difference?* Investopedia. https://www.investopedia.com/ask/answers/06/institutionalinvestor.asp

Parrish, K. (2022, April 28). *Increase Wi-Fi speed in 15 minutes without spending any money*. HighSpeedInternet. https://www.highspeedinternet.com/resources/improve-your-wi-fi-speed-in-10-simple-steps

Position sizing and risk management for beginners. (2022, January 3). Real Trading. https://realtrading.com/trading-blog/position-sizing-and-risk-management/

Potters, C. (2023, November 27). *Top 7 technical analysis tools*. Investopedia. https://www.investopedia.com/top-7-technical-analysis-tools-4773275

Putzhammer, M. (2022, June 28). *Crypto trading bots: The ultimate beginner's guide*. Trality Blog. https://www.trality.com/blog/crypto-trading-bots

Questions to determine your investment risk tolerance. (2023, January 6). USBank. https://www.usbank.com/financialiq/invest-your-money/

investment-strategies/whats-your-investment-risk-tolerance.html

Questions you need to ask yourself before you enter a trade. (2017, June 28). Orbex Forex Trading Blog. https://www.orbex.com/blog/en/2017/06/questions-you-need-ask-before-enter-trade

Rabin, K. (2024, February 13). *Should forex traders have an emergency fund?* Moneyshow. https://www.moneyshow.com/articles/tradingidea-56656/should-forex-traders-have-an-emergency-fund/

Rampe, T. (2017, March 8). *7 key benefits of day trading.* LinkedIn. https://www.linkedin.com/pulse/7-key-benefits-day-trading-todd-h-rampe/

Real. (2024). *Ladder option success stories: Real life examples of profitable trades.* FasterCapital. https://fastercapital.com/content/Ladder-option-success-stories--Real-life-examples-of-profitable-trades.html

Risk management strategies for advanced traders. (n.d.). AvaTrade. https://www.avatrade.com/education/online-trading-strategies/risk-management-strategies

Robinson, D. (2018, September 18). *5 criteria to consider when selecting stocks.* CNBC. https://www.cnbc.com/2018/09/18/5-criteria-to-consider-when-selecting-stocks.html

Rodeck, D. (2020, October 28). *Investing basics: Commodities trading guide.* Forbes Advisor. https://www.forbes.com/advisor/investing/commodities-trading/

Rolf. (2019, March 13). *6 tools for better stop loss placement.* Tradeciety; Quantum Trade Solutions GmbH. https://tradeciety.com/6-ways-to-place-stops-in-the-most-effective-way-pros-and-cons

Royal, J. (2023, December). *Long position vs. short position: What's the difference in stock trading?* Bankrate. https://www.bankrate.com/investing/long-and-short-stock-positions/

Royal, J. (2024, April 16). *Stock market basics: 9 tips for beginners.* Bankrate. https://www.bankrate.com/investing/stock-market-basics-for-beginners/#how-to-invest-in-the-stock-market

Sacchitello, M. (2019). *Best online brokers.* Investopedia. https://www.investopedia.com/best-online-brokers-4587872

Schwab, C. (2017, March 30). *How to determine your risk tolerance level.* Schwab Brokerage. https://www.schwab.com/learn/story/how-to-determine-your-risk-tolerance-level

Segal, T. (2024, June 21). *Fundamental analysis: Principles, types, and how to use it.* Investopedia. https://www.investopedia.com/terms/f/fundamentalanalysis.asp

Selecting ETFs. (2019). Schwab Brokerage. https://www.schwab.com/etfs/tools

Seth, S. (2019, August 17). *Choosing the right day-trading software.* Investopedia. https://www.investopedia.com/articles/active-trading/100714/vital-importance-choosing-right-day-trading-software.asp

Seth, S. (2023, March 21). *Basics of algorithmic trading: Concepts and examples.* Investopedia. https://www.investopedia.com/articles/active-trading/101014/basics-algorithmic-trading-concepts-and-examples.asp

Seven reasons why intraday traders lose money in the stock markets. (2024). Indiainfonline. https://www.indiainfoline.com/knowledge-center/trading-account/seven-reasons-why-intraday-traders-lose-money-in-the-stock-markets

Sigler, S. (n.d.). *Scott Sigler quote: "Choices have consequences."* Quotefancy. https://quotefancy.com/quote/2401450/Scott-Sigler-Choices-have-consequences

Six most important factors you should consider when choosing a broker. (2022, May 26). NewsnReleases. https://newsnreleases.com/2022/05/26/6-most-important-factors-you-should-consider-when-choosing-a-broker/

Six secret tips for supply and demand trading. (n.d.). Tradeciety. https://tradeciety.com/the-6-golden-rules-of-trading-supply-and-demand

Smusin, M. (2023, April 5). *How to build a trading bot.* Yellow Systems. https://yellow.systems/blog/how-to-build-a-trading-bot

Stephan, T. (2020, December 19). *Real-time watch list scanners - the complete guide.* Scanz. https://scanz.com/real-time-watchlist-scanners/

Sternlicht, L., & Sternlicht, A. (2024). *Top 10 myths about day trading addiction: Family addiction specialist: Addiction counselor.* Familyaddictionspecialist. https://www.familyaddictionspecialist.com/blog/top-10-myths-about-day-trading-addiction

The stop-loss order: Make sure you use it. (2024, March 3). Investopedia. https://www.investopedia.com/articles/stocks/09/use-stop-loss.asp

Strategy entry and exit rules. (2024). Tradestation. https://help.tradestation.com/10_00/eng/tradestationhelp/st/strategy_entry_exit_rules.htm

Stubbs, C. (2023, February 2). *Zero to A million: 15-Minute chart forex trading strategy.* Trading Strategy Guides. https://tradingstrategyguides.com/special-report-jacks-zero-to-a-million-trading-strategy/#google_vignette

Successful forex traders revealing their risk management strategies. (2020, May

24). The5ers Forex Prop Firm. https://the5ers.com/successful-forex-traders/

Supply and demand trading - strategy, rules etc. (n.d.). Angel One. https://www.angelone.in/knowledge-center/online-share-trading/supply-and-demand-trading

Sykes, T. (2018a, May 23). *8 advantages of day trading you need to know.* Timothy Sykes. https://www.timothysykes.com/blog/advantages-day-trading/

Sykes, T. (2018b, November 6). *6 crazy day trading myths versus reality.* Timothy Sykes. https://www.timothysykes.com/blog/day-trading-myths/

Sykes, T. (2021, July 26). *5 day trading success stories to inspire your journey.* Timothy Sykes. https://www.timothysykes.com/blog/day-trading-success-stories/

Sykes, T. (2023, May 15). *What are hot keys? The ultimate guide for day traders.* Timothy Sykes. https://www.timothysykes.com/blog/hot-keys/

Take all the advantages of litefinance. (2024). Litefinance. https://www.litefi nance.org/company/advantages/

Taube, S. (n.d.). *How to day trade.* NerdWallet. https://www.nerdwallet.com/article/investing/how-to-day-trade-safely

Technical analysis. (2011, March 17). BabyPips. https://www.babypips.com/learn/forex/technical-analysis

Teo, R. (2019, March 7). *The complete guide to stop loss order.* Tradingwith-Rayner. https://www.tradingwithrayner.com/stop-loss-order/

Teo, R. (2023, April 21). *How to set take profit orders (the essential guide).* TradingwithRayner. https://www.tradingwithrayner.com/take-profit-orders/

Theophanopoulos, A. (2018, December 28). *Top 7 reasons why forex traders fail and lose money.* Admirals. https://admiralmarkets.com/education/arti cles/trading-psychology/top-reasons-why-forex-traders-fail-and-lose-money

Three great reversal strategies for all timeframes. (2023, January 11). Tradeciety; Quantum Trade Solutions GmbH. https://tradeciety.com/3-great-rever sal-strategies

Three main types of risk in trading. (2023). Pepperstone. https://pepperstone.com/en-af/learn-to-trade/trading-guides/main-types-of-risk-in-trad ing/

Three types of forex charts and how to read them. (2021, April 25). BabyPips. https://www.babypips.com/learn/forex/types-of-charts

Three working 5-minute trading strategies. (2023, January 10). Market Pulse. https://fxopen.com/blog/en/three-working-5-minute-trading-strategies/

Top 30 most famous day traders and their secrets to success. (2022, August 31). TOP1 Markets. https://www.top1markets.com/insights/Stocks/famous-day-traders

Toyco, J. (2023, August 3). *The complete guide to trend following strategies*. TradingwithRayner. https://www.tradingwithrayner.com/trend-following-strategies/

Trading according to the real market? (2024). Thefundedtraderprogram. https://help.thefundedtraderprogram.com/en/articles/5374175-trading-according-to-the-real-market

Tristan, D. (2023). *One hour trading strategy for beginners*. Brokerxplorer; Brokerxplorer.com. https://www.brokerxplorer.com/article/1hour-trading-strategy-for-beginners-4257

Tuli, P. (2019, May 30). *Here's why stock traders need fast internet*. Justdial; Justdial Blog. https://www.justdial.com/JDSocialBlog/Broadband-Internet-Service-Providers/Heres-Why-Stock-Traders-Need-Fast-Internet/421915355413

Vipond, T. (n.d.). *Long and short positions*. Corporate Finance Institute. https://corporatefinanceinstitute.com/resources/career-map/sell-side/capital-markets/long-and-short-positions/

Vipond, T. (2024). *Technical analysis: A beginner's guide*. Corporate Finance Institute. https://corporatefinanceinstitute.com/resources/career-map/sell-side/capital-markets/technical-analysis/

What are indices? (n.d.). IG. https://www.ig.com/en/indices/what-are-indices-how-do-you-trade-them

What are indices? The beginner's guide. (2024, October 29). AvaTrade. https://www.avatrade.com/indices/what-are-indices

What are indices? A beginner's guide to indices trading. (2024, August 29). EToro. https://www.etoro.com/trading/guide-to-trading-indices/

What happens when you ignore risk. (2022). TheFamilyOffice. https://tfoco.com/en/insights/articles/what-happens-when-investors-ignore-risk

What is a trader's community? (2023, April 11). Medium. https://medium.com/@stockedge_/what-is-a-traders-community-4f8e9611b299

What is a trading edge and why do I need one? (2024). CMCmarkets. https://www.cmcmarkets.com/en/trading-guides/trading-edge

What is high-frequency trading? (2019). Investopedia. https://www.investopedia.com/ask/answers/09/high-frequency-trading.asp

What is paper trading? Advantages & disadvantages. (2023, December 27). AvaTrade. https://www.avatrade.com/education/correct-trading-rules/paper-trading

What is stop loss (SL) and take profit (TP) and how to use it? (2023, November 7). Axiory. https://www.axiory.com/trading-resources/trading-terms/stop-loss-take-profit

What is the difference between retail traders & institutional traders? (2022, May 12). Bookmap. https://bookmap.com/blog/what-is-the-difference-between-retail-institutional-traders

What is trade risk? Know about factors, impacts, and strategies. (n.d.). Corporate. https://www.allianz-trade.com/en_HK/insights/risk-management/what-is-trade-risk.html

What is trading edge and why its important for a trader? (2023). Tradingcoach. https://tradingcoach.co.in/what-is-trading-edge-why-is-it-important/

Why most traders lose money: 24 surprising statistics. (2019, February 9). Tradeciety. https://tradeciety.com/24-statistics-why-most-traders-lose-money

Why stock traders need fast internet. (2022, December 21). Actcorp. https://www.actcorp.in/blog/why-stock-traders-need-fast-internet

The winning mindset of a trader. (n.d.). Corporate Finance Institute. https://corporatefinanceinstitute.com/resources/career-map/sell-side/capital-markets/winning-mindset-of-a-trader/

Wohlner, R. (2023, February 14). *10 best technical analysis software for trading*. Money. https://money.com/best-technical-analysis-software-for-trading/

Woods, G. (2016, December 20). *10 steps to creating your first trading strategy*. Trading Setups Review. https://www.tradingsetupsreview.com/10-steps-creating-first-trading-strategy/

Yazdanparast, E. (2021, November 7). *How to set take profit and stop loss orders at the same time*. Medium; Coinmonks. https://medium.com/coinmonks/how-to-set-take-profit-and-stop-loss-orders-at-the-same-time-303080e666a9

Yochim, D. (2019, January 29). *9 best online brokers for stock trading of December 2019*. NerdWallet. https://www.nerdwallet.com/best/investing/online-brokers-for-stock-trading

Zucchi, K. (4 C.E., October 21). *Four steps to picking A stock*. Investopedia. https://www.investopedia.com/articles/stocks/09/screening-stocks-for-investing.asp

Zucchi, K. (2021, August 18). *Institutional traders vs. retail traders: What's the difference?* Investopedia. https://www.investopedia.com/articles/active-trading/030515/what-difference-between-institutional-traders-and-retail-traders.asp

Image References

AlphaTradeZone. (2020). *A notebook and smartphone on the table* [Image]. Pexels. https://www.pexels.com/photo/a-notebook-and-smartphone-on-the-table-5831670/

Bell, D. (2019). *Silver iPhone* [Image]. Pexels. https://www.pexels.com/photo/silver-iphone-2068664/

Chisu, R. (2019). *Low-angle photography of-man in the-middle of building* [Image]. Unsplash. https://unsplash.com/photos/low-angle-photography-of-man-in-the-middle-of-buidligns-Ua-agENjmI4

Diesel, A. (2019). *Person using MacBook pro* [Image]. Unsplash. https://unsplash.com/photos/person-using-macbook-pro-744oGeqpxPQ

Graham, S. (2016). *Person holding pencil near laptop* [Image]. Unsplash. https://unsplash.com/photos/person-holding-pencil-near-laptop-computer-5fNmWej4tAA

Krakenimages. (2020). *Two middle age business workers smiling happy and confident. working together with smile on face hand giving high five at the office* [Image]. Unsplash. https://unsplash.com/photos/man-in-white-dress-shirt-sitting-beside-woman-in-black-long-sleeve-shirt-376KN_ISplE

Krukau, Y. (2021). *Person holding a black smartphone* [Image]. Pexels. https://www.pexels.com/photo/person-in-gray-long-sleeve-shirt-holding-black-smartphone-7693221/

Miroshnichenko, T. (2021a). *A person holding a smartphone* [Image]. Pexels. https://www.pexels.com/photo/a-person-holding-a-smartphone-7567228/

Miroshnichenko, T. (2021b). *Analysis, analyst, analytics* [Image]. Pexels. https://www.pexels.com/photo/marketing-man-laptop-internet-7567236/

Nekrashevich, A. (2012). *Business, paper, finance* [Image]. Pexels. https://www.pexels.com/photo/business-paper-finance-decision-6801651/

Piacquadio, A. (2020). *Man showing distress* [Image]. Pexels. https://www.pexels.com/photo/man-showing-distress-3777572/

Pixabay. (2016). *Macbook pro on table* [Image]. Pexels. https://www.pexels.com/photo/macbook-pro-on-table-259091/

Street, J. (2020). *Black android smartphone on brown wooden table* [Image].

Unsplash. https://unsplash.com/photos/black-android-smartphone-on-brown-wooden-table-VP4WmibxvcY

TheFirst, L. (2021a). *Smartphone displaying a stock market chart lying on documents next to a laptop on the desk* [Image]. Pexels. https://www.pexels.com/photo/smartphone-displaying-a-stock-market-chart-lying-on-documents-next-to-a-laptop-on-the-desk-7887850/

TheFirst, L. (2021b). *Smartphone on a table* [Image]. Pexels. https://www.pexels.com/photo/smartphone-on-the-table-7887817/

TheWeekender, B. (2016). *Graph on an iPad* [Image]. Pexels. https://www.pexels.com/photo/graphs-display-on-an-ipad-187041/

Traxer. (2012). *A pile of gold and silver bitcoins* [Image]. Unsplash. https://unsplash.com/photos/a-pile-of-gold-and-silver-bitcoins-kM6QNrgo0YE

Vaitkevich, N. (2020). *Black smartphone on white paper* [Image]. Pexels. https://www.pexels.com/photo/black-smartphone-on-white-paper-6120182/

Winkler, M. (2024). *The word-trading spelled out in scrabble letters* [Image]. Pexels. https://www.pexels.com/photo/the-word-trading-spelled-out-in-scrabble-letters-19825348/

Żerdzicki, J. (2024). *An iPhone sitting on top of a table* [Image]. Unsplash. https://unsplash.com/photos/a-remote-control-sitting-on-top-of-a-table-ip7GFn5JqX8

www.ingramcontent.com/pod-product-compliance
Lightning Source LLC
LaVergne TN
LVHW022214200926
848481LV00006B/1959
9781919168302